SEX IN PRISON

SEX IN PRISON

MYTHS AND REALITIES

edited by
Catherine D. Marcum
Tammy L. Castle

LYNNE
RIENNER
PUBLISHERS

BOULDER
LONDON

Published in the United States of America in 2014 by
Lynne Rienner Publishers, Inc.
1800 30th Street, Boulder, Colorado 80301
www.rienner.com

and in the United Kingdom by
Lynne Rienner Publishers, Inc.
3 Henrietta Street, Covent Garden, London WC2E 8LU

Library of Congress Cataloging-in-Publication Data
Sex in prison : myths and realities / [edited by] Catherine D. Marcum
  and Tammy L. Castle.
    p. cm.
  Includes bibliographical references and index.
  ISBN 978-1-62637-030-2 (hc : alk. paper)
  1. Prisoners—Sexual behavior. 2. Prisoners—Social conditions.
I. Marcum, Catherine Davis, 1980–   II. Castle, Tammy L.
  HV8836.S46 2014
  365'.6—dc23
                                                      2013016462

British Cataloguing in Publication Data
A Cataloguing in Publication record for this book
is available from the British Library.

Printed and bound in the United States of America

ⓧ   The paper used in this publication meets the requirements
     of the American National Standard for Permanence of
     Paper for Printed Library Materials Z39.48-1992.

     5 4 3 2 1

Contents

Acknowledgments

We would like to thank Andrew Berzanskis and the staff at Lynne Rienner Publishers for their efficient and effective help throughout the publication process. We would also like to thank the volume contributors for their hard work here, as well as their continued research on this taboo but important subject.

Catherine D. Marcum: I would like to thank my fantastic coeditor, Tammy Castle, for all of her hard work and collaboration on this project. Also, I'd like to thank my nephews—Zach, Nick, Chase, and Gabe—for the humor and entertainment they have provided me throughout their lives. I love you and am proud to be your aunt.

Tammy L. Castle: I would like to thank my coeditor, Catherine Marcum, for the initial project impetus and for her diligence in shepherding the project throughout the process.

1

Examining Prison Sex Culture

Catherine D. Marcum

Inmates live very different lives compared to individuals outside prison walls. Every move they make within a twenty-four-hour period is regulated and supervised. Trips to the bathroom, recreation time, and eating lunch, such simple activities, are constantly monitored by corrections officers. Termed "total institutions" (Goffman, 1961), prisons are closed facilities that separate individuals from society. Everything an inmate does is performed inside a prison without break. They are same-sex societies, which makes being in them even more of an adjustment from living in a free world with access to both sexes and other opportunities. Further, residents share all aspects of their lives with the others in that facility (Hensley et al., 2003). As interaction with family and friends during incarceration is limited, if even existent, inmates will often become emotionally and physically dependent on each other in many ways.

Although portions of their life are extremely regulated while incarcerated, inmates do hold control over their emotional and mental selves. In other words, total institutions cannot control values, beliefs, and norms of social roles of inmates, nor can they prevent them from sharing these mores with other inmates. Prison subcultures are formed within the facilities as a result of these shared values. For example, a group within the prison may worship Judaism together and uphold those values. Or another group may support the beliefs of a particularly violent gang and still practice those values while incarcerated. Further, the formation of this subculture is a means of mitigating a sense of social rejection as a result of incarceration as well as a way to rebel against the norms and values of normative society (Bondesson, 1989; Irwin, 1980; Sykes, 1958). Inmates who are incarcerated can commiserate with others inside prison walls rather than experience the potential shunning of those on the outside.

When inmates enter prison, they begin to adapt to the prison lifestyle and the subcultures that are present. According to Einat and Einat (2000), they are participating in the concept of "prisonization." Multiple researchers have attempted to provide theoretical explanations of the adjustment and behavior of prison inmates (Clemmer, 1940; Irwin and Cressey, 1962; Sykes, 1958; Toch, 1977), with two main theories receiving the most support. The deprivation model asserts that deprivations (or losses of liberties) experienced in prison are the main influence on an individual's response to incarceration. According to Sykes (1958), five main pains (or losses) result from imprisonment:

1. Liberty and freedoms available to those not incarcerated.
2. Goods and services, ranging from choosing a grocery store to picking a mechanic.
3. Heterosexual relationships with men and women of an individual's choice.
4. Autonomy and self-sufficiency.
5. Security and protection from harm.

As a mechanism for coping with the loss of these freedoms and liberties, the inmates form a new set of values and norms, some of which lead to inappropriate behavior during incarceration (Marcum, Hilinski, and Freiburger, forthcoming). For example, individuals on the outside have the freedom to participate in heterosexual relationships at their leisure. As incarceration only allows the cohabitation of others of the same sex, many inmates choose to participate in homosexual relationships, an activity that is banned in prison.

The second theoretical frame of thought, the importation model, suggests the inmates bring in norms, values, and beliefs held prior to incarceration, and this transference of prior ideals influences their behavior (Irwin and Cressey, 1962). In other words, religious preferences, gang affiliations, and family values continue to be an integral part of inmates' lives even after incarceration, and they bring those values in with them to the facility. Inmates do not stop believing in the Jewish faith or supporting the mores and values of the Latin Kings just because they become incarcerated—all of these personal affiliations go with them. Further, these personal characteristics are likely to have influenced their involvement in crime before arrest and affect their behavior while incarcerated. Gang affiliation provides a classic example, as corrections officials are constantly trying to separate gang members to prevent altercations and riots while they are incarcerated, as well as to intercept communication to members on the outside.

Prison Argot

Despite the influential factors of the development of the prison subculture, it is evident that it exists. And, as common with all subcultures, a language is utilized in this total institution. While the majority of the inmates have English as a first language, a language or slang is also developed within prison walls. This language, referred to as prison argot, is distinct from the language of noninmates (Hensley et al., 2003) and is functional for inmates. It is representative of a collective stand of coping with prison life and its deprivations (Goffman, 1961). As mentioned previously, incarceration results in deprivation of certain freedoms, but also leads to uncomfortable living conditions, boredom, uncertainty about the future, and adaptation to the types of peers present in the prison environment (Farrington, 1994; Toch, 1992). Much like how children use "pig Latin" or other secret codes to communicate to avoid detection by parental supervision, inmates have developed argot to use as a distinct language.

    Language itself is an important method of communication, as well as a key component in socialization and development of behavioral codes (Dean-Brown, 1993; Dietrich and Graumann, 1989). Different cultures and subcultures can be identified by the language they use. Inmates can be identified by the slang they use while incarcerated, and it identifies the needs and interests of the group (Hensley et al., 2002). According to Einat and Einat (2000), prison argot has six functions:

1. Uniqueness, as a distinct language allows a person to stand out.
2. Alleviation of feelings of rejection by individuals on the outside, whether friends, family, or general society.
3. Development of relationships with other incarcerated inmates within the facility.
4. Declaration of membership in the subculture, as proficiency in a language indicates affiliation with a society.
5. Identification tool indicating acceptance by a group, as only inmates are authorized to use prison argot.
6. Secrecy.

Prison argot allows for roles to be developed within the prison societies and for hierarchies of social status to be developed. It also indicates the level of respect the inmate has from other inmates and staff members (Dumond, 1992). These roles do not exclude prison sexual hierarchy, as a structure of roles is associated with sexual activities within prison walls. Males and females often adapt to prison life in different ways, including formation of sexual relationships. For instance, men often participate in sexual relationships as a method of obtaining protection from more feared inmates, while women participate in these relationships to gain companionship or form a pseudo-family atmosphere. In turn, the prison argot associated with sexual habits of inmates defines their role (e.g., "father/uncle," indicating a dominating role in a female family, or "fag," indicating a submissive role in a male relationship).

In 1934, Joseph Fishman conducted one of the first studies on sex in a male prison facility (Hensley et al., 2003). At that time, homosexuality was a criminal offense. Men were sent to prisons, such as the Welfare Island Penitentiary in New York, to serve time for sexual offenses such as homosexuality, corruption of a minor, and purchasing sex from another man. These men were termed "fags" or "fairies" and wore feminine-type apparel and makeup. Aggressive inmates, labeled as "wolves" or "top men," took advantage of these more feminine male inmates and targeted them for sexual victimization. Although research between 1934 and now has expanded, the same basic trend has maintained itself in the prison system regarding aggressive inmates and passive inmates. A multitude of researchers (Donaldson, 1993a; Sagarin, 1976; Sykes, 1958) even went to the extent of labeling inmates who participate in homosexual activity into a continuum of categories, ranging from the masculine aggressors (aka "daddies") to the passive feminines (aka "punks" or "fags").

Sexual aggressors, or "wolves," in prison facilities focus on proving masculinity and machismo in order to become the dominant force in a sexual relationship. "Wolves" assume the role not only to obtain the physical release associated with sex but also to establish a reputation and avoid victimization. Although they are participating in homosexual relationships (whether consensually or through force), they are not labeled as such and instead earn a high place in the institutional hierarchy (Donaldson, 1993a; Kirkham, 1971). Their ability to dominate other men is not considered a manner of sexual preference, but an issue of manliness and strength.

There are two main roles the other counterpart of the homosexual relationship can take. "Fags" (or the passive individuals in the homosexual relationship) are stereotyped by other inmates as playing a natural role and assumed to be the same way on the outside. They are feminine and flamboyant, therefore not a threat to other masculine inmates. According to Donaldson (1993a), "fags" were indicated as having "pussies" and not "assholes" and wore blouses and not shirts. Although these individuals (or "queens") do not earn as much "respect" as the "wolves," they do earn some as they are assuming a natural role. In other words, they are given some credit for accepting the role as the passive male in the relationship. On the other hand, "punks" or "jailhouse turnouts" are given to inmates for the purpose of forcible sex (rape). They do not display feminine characteristics as "fags" do and are not respected as they are viewed as cowards who are weak and unable to defend themselves. Hensley and colleagues (2003) stated they are men who cannot fulfill the role of a man. Further, Donaldson (1993a) asserted these men were generally younger, first-time offenders, white, and smaller in stature. Kirkham (1971) called them "canteen punks" as they were not only used for sex, but more for goods and services (much like a prostitute).

Wooden and Parker (1982) went even further to explain argot sexual roles by distinguishing between the actual physical altercation, so who was the insertor and insertee. The insertee can be either a homosexual or a weaker heterosexual. Often referred to as "broads," "bitches," or "sissies," insertees were suggested to take on the feminine roles and even names. The insertors were those who had masculine personas that were referred to as "stud," "straight who uses," or "jockers." Calling a man a "jocker" generally indicated he was a rapist, but as this behavior is situational in prison, it is accepted. A male who assumes this role in the sexual relationship is assumed to be the stronger and more dominant individual.

Sexual Behaviors in Prison

As discussed previously, incarceration results in a loss of many freedoms and liberties. Participation in sexual relationships with others is one of those liberties, a behavior that is of extreme importance to many. Although participation in sexual relationships is forbidden in correctional facilities, correctional administration cannot prevent prisoners from being consumed with sex (Money and Bohmer, 1980). As a result of the sexual deprivation they experience, prisoners may seek relief in alternative ways (Worley and Worley, 2013).

Participating in autoerotism is often a behavior inmates will choose to relieve sexual tension. Of the few studies done on this behavior, it appears to be acceptable among the inmate population. Wooden and Parker (1982) found that every inmate in their study reported masturbating while incarcerated, with 46 percent masturbating three to five times per week and 14 percent masturbating daily. Furthermore, Hensley, Tewksbury, and Koscheski (2001) found that 99.3 percent of their male inmate sample reported masturbating while incarcerated. Interestingly enough, the more educated inmates were more likely to be frequent masturbators. Although Hensley, Tewksbury, and Wright (2001) found that less female inmates admitted to the behavior, a large portion (66.5 percent) of female inmates in a southern facility participated in regular masturbation.

Inmates know this behavior is normally forbidden during incarceration. However, research has indicated that male inmates will rationalize this behavior in order to continue to participate in masturbation. Worley and Worley (2013) tested this behavior with Sykes and Matza's neutralization theory, which has been used to explain many types of criminal behavior, such as shoplifting (Cromwell and Thurman, 2003), digital piracy (Morris and Higgins, 2009), and sex trafficking (Antonopoulos and Winterdyk, 2005). They questioned male inmates about their behaviors and the effect on female correctional officers in the prison. Worley and Worley found that, when participating in autoerotism in prison, inmates will usually justify the behavior by denying an injury took place, stating that no one was harmed or the female staff members enjoyed the display. Many inmates denied a victim in the instance, stating either females did not belong in a prison setting so they got their just deserts, or by working at a prison they obviously wanted to see male genitalia. With either form of neutralization used, the responsibility was removed from the male and often placed on the legitimately employed female staff member.

Inmates will also use masturbation to establish inappropriate relationships with correctional officers (Dial and Worley, 2008). If an inmate masturbates openly and the behavior is ignored by the staff member, the passive acquiescence is perceived as a go-ahead to establish a relationship. However, if the staff member chastises the inmate for the behavior, the rebuke indicates the staff member is not interested in a relationship, and the inmate will pretend the behavior was "an accident."

Some inmates will persist in attempts to participate in inappropriate relationships with correctional staff, despite rejection by the staff. Allen and Bosta (1981) asserted that these offenders can be placed into five categories, and this process involves an intricate system of information gathering and actions:

1. *Observers* monitor correctional staff to determine who would be the most likely to be manipulated into these relationships and then release this information to those inmates who will actually perform the manipulation.
2. *Contacts* obtain personal information about staff and turn it over to other inmates.
3. *Runners* test staff members to gauge determination of the officer to enforce rules, such as asking for a candy bar or extra food at lunch.
4. *Point men* are the lookouts for the inmates who participate in the manipulation.
5. *Turners* attempt to befriend employees and manipulate them into inappropriate behaviors.

Turners can also be separated into three categories: (1) heartbreakers, who seek to form emotional bonds; (2) exploiters, who use employees to get what they want, such as contraband or information; and (3) hell-raisers, who use relationships to create problems (Worley, Marquart, and Mullings, 2003).

While the majority of correctional facilities have rules against public autoerotism, this behavior still occurs in prison, sometimes to the point of creating an adverse environment for inmates and correctional staff. In *Beckford v. Department of Corrections* (2010), a federal appellate court ruled that the Florida Department of Corrections failed to fix a hostile work environment for female health-care workers and correctional staff. Male inmates in maximum security continuously masturbated in the presence of fourteen female employees over the course of three years. They would participate in "gunning," where the inmates openly masturbated in the presence of the employees by standing on toilets or mattresses to ensure the victims could see the behavior. They would ejaculate through the food slot on their doors. The staff resorted to wearing sunglasses and headphones to avoid the harassment, as the Department of Corrections refused to attempt to amend the inmates' behavior.

Many inmates who participate in sexual relationships with other same-sex inmates during incarceration do not identify themselves as homosexuals (Hensley, Tewksbury, and Wright, 2001). In what is termed *situational homosexuality,* individuals who are immersed in single-sex environments resort to same-sex sexual activity to relieve desires with the understanding they will return to heterosexual sexual activities once removed from the segregated environment (Sagarin, 1976). Ibrahim (1974), one of the first researchers to examine situational homosexuality, determined that six factors within the structure of a prison contribute to this behavior:

1. A prison is a sex-segregated community and sexual gratification can only be achieved through a person of the same sex.
2. Although the behavior is forbidden and regulated, it is often tolerated by corrections officers and other inmates. This passive acceptance encourages the creation of status roles, where some inmates are assigned more masculine identities while others are seen as weaker.
3. Insufficient work opportunities lead to boredom and idle time for long periods. Inmates who work are kept busy and are less likely to participate in deviant behaviors.

4. Overcrowding of prisons causes close quarters for inmates, in which they watch each other change clothes and use the bathroom. Older inmates often take advantage of this situation with the younger inmates.
5. The current classification system of inmates does not segregate individuals based on sexual preference.
6. Complete isolation from the outside world and the norms of society can influence inmates to develop their own norms, one of those entailing sexual interaction with other inmates.

Data Collection

Gathering accurate data from inmates regarding any form of behavior or lifestyle characteristic can be extremely difficult. First, accessing this protected population can be a challenge for any researcher. Even if access is granted by the appropriate administration, the utmost importance is placed on prison safety, so a scheduled appointment at a facility can be cancelled without prior notice. However, the second issue that can present itself is obtaining honest answers from the inmates. Inmates can be hesitant in answering questions about offending behaviors (or even victimization) for fear of punishment or retaliation. Inmates are extremely distrustful, so even if the research assures anonymity, inmates will assume their behaviors will be immediately reported to administration. Or inmates may answer dishonestly to rebel against participation in a study or to make themselves look like more impressive offenders. With that being said, research performed on sexual relationships in prison has produced varied results.

A stereotypical assumption suggests that entrance into an incarcerating facility as a resident (aka inmate) equates to a guaranteed experience with sexual victimization. In other words, a societal assumption exists that a person will be raped while incarcerated. Although the fear of sexual victimization while incarcerated is actually more common than the actual occurrence (Tewksbury, 1989a), it is becoming a prevalent problem for our corrections system. Early assertions of the occurrence of sexual assault during incarceration were speculative as gaining access to prisons to conduct research is difficult.

Multiple recent studies have indicated that, while it may not be as prevalent as Hollywood and myth would have us believe, inmate rape is widespread and underreported (Dumond, 2003; Hensley, 2002; Hensley et al., 2002; Hensley, Koscheski, and Tewksbury, 2003; Struckman-Johnson and Struckman-Johnson, 2000). While as early as the 1930s rape was recognized as an issue (Fishman, 1934), it was not until 2003 that President George W. Bush signed the Prison Rape Elimination Act (PREA) into law (Bureau of Justice Statistics, 2004) to address this noted form of victimization within prison walls. PREA addressed the increasing problem of prison rape by creating a zero-tolerance policy for sexual assaults in the correctional system, providing funding for research and programs, and requiring data collection on rape and assault. Since the implementation of PREA, punishment for those perpetrators of sexual assault has increased in severity. Inmate perpetrators may be relocated to a more secure facility or placed in solitary confinement. Staff perpetrators can be fired from their positions or even criminally prosecuted. Furthermore, PREA requires the Bureau of Justice Statistics to annually report occurrences of sexual victimization of inmates perpetrated by inmates and other staff members. While obtaining a precise number of occurrences is difficult due to the issues noted above, the requirements of PREA are a positive step in regard to the development of prevention policies.

Reported rates of sexual assault inside correctional facilities have varied from 1 percent to 41 percent (Wolff and Shi, 2008), generally due to two factors: (1) the underreporting of occurrences, which is attributed to the stigma of being assaulted and fear of retribution (Eigenberg, 2000; Struckman-Johnson et al., 1996) and (2) methodology variances in regard to what is considered sexual assault (Beck and Harrison, 2007a; Struckman-Johnson and Struckman-Johnson, 2006; Wolff and Shi, 2009). For example, Beck and Harrison (2007a) found that the average rate of rape is below 5 percent, but the between-facility rates vary from 0 percent to 12 percent (Wolff et al., 2006). The first report by the Bureau of Justice Statistics reported 8,210 allegations of sexual violence within prison walls nationwide, but only 2,100 of the allegations (30 percent) were substantiated.

The Bureau of Justice Statistics also reports sexual victimization occurrences specifically relating to jails. They have found among the 40,419 jail inmates participating in the survey, 3.2 percent experienced one or more incidents of sexual victimization (Beck and Harrison, 2008). Almost 2 percent reported an incident involving another inmate. In regard to predictors of the victimization, the report asserted that sexual victimization in jails was not related to facility characteristics but inmate characteristics. In other words, inmate characteristics such as criminal history, violence factors, and age are significantly related to sexual assault compared to the organization and population of the jail facility.

Some of the research in the field is directly aimed at exploring inmate-on-inmate sexual victimization. For example, Hensley, Castle, and Tewksbury (2003) surveyed female inmates in a southern correctional facility and found that of the respondents (n = 245), 4.5 percent reported incidents of sexual coercion while 2.0 percent admitted to perpetrating the incidents against another inmate. Wolff and Shi (2008) recently investigated occurrences of inmate-on-inmate sexual victimization at thirteen facilities in one state. Of the 6,964 male inmates surveyed, 4 percent reported some form of sexual victimization perpetrated by another inmate. Victimization was more frequently reported by females (n = 564), at a rate of 22 percent. The most common form of victimization was categorized as abusive sexual contact, which involved sexually inappropriate touching, and was not frequently reported to prison authorities. Nonconsensual sexual acts (i.e., sexual assault or rape) between inmates were rare (less than 2 percent), but much more likely to be reported to prison authorities. Furthermore, 75 percent of the male inmates who reported victimization stated they had experienced one to three forms of the victimization, while 95 percent of the reported female victims claimed experiencing one to three forms of the victimization.

Examining Prison Sex Culture

Our purpose in this book is to provide the reader an updated and accurate examination of the prison sex culture in the United States, as well as comparing our current state with other nations. The contributors of this book are scholars in the field with extensive expertise on this topic, and combined, they provide a thorough review of the contemporary issues of prison sex behaviors. Listed below is a brief description of each chapter.

In Chapter 2, Kristine Levan discusses the consensual sexual relationships in prison and the dynamic that is involved. Conversely,

Richard Tewksbury and David P. Connor examine nonconsensual relationships in prison in Chapter 3. While sex in prison is illegal, whether consensual or forced, it affects the entire prison experience for inmates in regard to safety, commerce, and emotions. Barbara Zaitzow examines in Chapter 4 the corrections system's response to the tension caused by this situation and gives suggestions to assist victims and prevent future occurrence.

The next few chapters present information on the repercussions of participating in any sexual relationship in prison. In Chapter 5, Tammy L. Castle discusses conjugal visitation and marriage of an inmate to an individual outside the prison walls, and how our corrections system handles these particular instances. In Chapter 6, Ashley G. Blackburn, Shannon L. Fowler, and Janet L. Mullings address the notion of gender role sexuality and the adaptation process of new and existing inmates in the prison environment. Roberto Hugh Potter and Jeffrey Rosky examine, in Chapter 7, health issues associated with participation in a sexual relationship in any venue, specifically sexually transmitted diseases (STDs), the human immunodeficiency virus (HIV), acquired immune deficiency syndrome (AIDS), and pregnancy. And in Chapter 8, Tomer Einat provides the reader with an international perspective on prison sex and a comparison of the United States with other countries around the world.

The remaining chapters serve to address special issues associated with sex in prison. In Chapter 9, Danielle McDonald and Alexis Miller offer a special case study investigating the effect of PREA on female inmates in a correctional facility in Kentucky, which allows the reader to see a real-world application of existing legislation. Finally, the editors conclude with Chapter 10, a policy implication review of the material presented in the previous chapters.

We believe this book will be an asset to academics and practitioners alike as it will demonstrate how our corrections system is evolving and adapting to this pressing issue. As you read, please consider the past and current states of the issue and if our corrections system is effectively addressing the needs of inmates, as well as providing effective punishment to deter future inappropriate and illegal behavior.

2

Consensual Sex

Kristine Levan

Early literature on sexual activities among inmates often dismissed the issue by making the simple observation that correctional institutions are "a fertile field for the development of sex abnormalities" (Clemmer, 1958, p. 249). By making assumptions about sexual activity behind bars, these early studies helped to perpetuate the myth that sexual activities that inmates engage in are primarily consensual and homosexual. As I will illustrate in this chapter, consensual sexual activity occurs between both male and female inmates, as well as inmates and staff, and it occurs among inmates who consider themselves to be homosexual, bisexual, and heterosexual.

Much of the recent correctional research and policymaking focus has been geared toward prevention of sexual assault and rape among prison populations. Considerably less attention has been given to nonviolent sexual activities. Examining consensual sexual activities is equally important. First, the lines between consensual, coercive, and violent sexual activities are often blurred and those who engage in what may at first seem like consensual sexual activities may be subjected to similar emotional and physical injuries as those who are violently victimized. The concept of consensual sex is a tenuous one. Among inmates, the prison argot dictates that some inmates are dominant over others. Sex between inmates and correctional staff can really never be considered completely consensual, as the power differential always exists between the two. Additionally, those who engage in any form of sexual activity risk contracting sexually transmitted diseases, including hepatitis C, HIV, and AIDS.

The frequency of consensual sex is elusive. Researchers have gathered varying rates of the prevalence of consensual sex. For instance, Wooden and Parker (1982) indicate that 65 percent of their sample had engaged in some form of consensual sex with another inmate while incarcerated. Other studies indicate that as few as 2 percent of the inmates in their sample had engaged in similar behaviors (Saum et al., 1995).

Inmate Consensual Sex in Male Institutions

The male prison environment is one that has historically been rife with interpersonal violence, both among inmates and between inmates and correctional staff. For instance, the original tenets of the convict code, as identified by Sykes (1958), emphasize ideals such as toughness and masculinity, while encouraging inmates to be loyal to one another. Within these tenets lies some explanation behind consensual sex as well. One method, by which male inmates express their masculinity, in the absence of females, is to become the dominant sexual partner. As such, male inmates may self-identify as either situationally or dispositionally homosexual, which are characteristics generally used to determine their place on the prison sexual hierarchy.

Situational vs. Dispositional Homosexuality

The majority of inmates do not self-identify as homosexual. Those who are homosexual or bisexual in the community are likely to import their attitudes and behaviors into the correctional setting; these individuals would be likely to engage in homosexual sex, regardless of whether or not they are institutionalized. This prior inclination is categorized as being dispositionally homosexual or bisexual.

In contrast, some inmates engage in homosexual activity while they are incarcerated as a result of being institutionalized exclusively with others of the same sex. This changing identity is known as situational homosexuality. One of the deprivations of imprisonment, a loss of heterosexual relationships, reflects the importance that is placed on sexual relations (Sykes, 1958). As a result of this loss, many inmates engage in sexual activity with members of the same sex while incarcerated, reverting to heterosexual relationships upon their release back to the community. Situational homosexual activities comprise the majority of sexual activities occurring among inmates (Fleisher and Krienert, 2009; Ibrahim, 1974).

Situational homosexuality is illustrated in Hensley's (2000a) study on consensual sexual activity. The majority of inmates surveyed (80 percent) considered themselves to be heterosexual. Despite this, one-fifth of those surveyed had engaged in anal sex with other inmates. Nearly one-fourth had either touched another inmate's penis or had allowed their penis to be touched by another inmate. Approximately one-fourth of those surveyed had either received or given oral sex to another inmate. Inmates' sexual activities seem not to reflect whether they self-identify as homosexual or bisexual, despite the importance placed on their sexual orientation while they are incarcerated.

Fleisher and Krienert's (2009) study supported the idea that most sexual activity within prisons is consensual. Based on 564 interviews with male and female inmates in thirty correctional institutions throughout the country, the authors found that most inmates did not worry about nonconsensual sexual activity because sex was readily available. Inmates reported that plenty of opportunities exist for voluntary sexual activity within all prisons.

The Prison Sexual Hierarchy and Argot Roles

An inmate's place in the prison sexual hierarchy is partially determined by his or her sexual orientation, both inside and outside of the institution (Dumond, 1992). At the top of the hierarchy are those inmates that are considered "wolves." While these inmates may engage in sexually aggressive acts against other inmates, they are also known to engage in consensual sex with others, typically adopting the dominant role in the activity. Because they are the more aggressive and dominant party in the exchange, "wolves" avoid the negative stigmatization associated with more submissive same-sex activities (Donaldson, 1993b; Hensley et al., 2003; Sykes, 1958).

In their 2003 study on prison argot roles, Hensley and his colleagues further expanded the "wolves" category to include two subcategories. "Aggressive wolves" are more likely to engage in sexual violence than consensual sex and are more likely to limit their activities to more dominant roles. "Nonaggressive wolves" typically seek those who are willing to engage in consensual sex with them and are less likely to resort to sexually violent behavior. Similarly to the aggressive subcategory, they typically partake in more dominant roles during sex. However, they are more likely to self-identify as situationally bisexual than the "aggressive wolves."

The second tier of the sexual hierarchy is made up of "fags." These inmates are dispositionally homosexual and are reasonably well respected by "wolves." They often engage in consensual sex with each other or with members of other tiers of the hierarchy. Additionally, they often adopt more feminine roles, including cleaning inmates' cells, washing laundry, or growing their hair long (Donaldson, 1993a; Hensley et al., 2003; Man and Cronan, 2002).

More nuanced subcategories have also been cited for the "fag" category. Those belonging to the "fish" subcategory are openly homosexual and adopt less dominant roles during sexual activity. In contrast, those who consider themselves "closeted gays" are secretly homosexual upon admission to prison and may adopt either dominant or submissive roles during sex. While the "fish" adopt feminine characteristics, "closeted gays" maintain their more masculine identities and often seek out other closeted inmates to build relationships with (Hensley et al., 2003).

The final tier of the prison hierarchy is comprised of "punks." These inmates are situationally homosexual and engage in various forms of sex with other inmates (consensual, coercive, and violent), usually with "wolves." Often the consensual sex is in exchange for protection or other favors (Donaldson, 1993b). "Punks" are among the least respected inmates, as they are seen as weak (Hensley et al., 2003). As such, they may be used as commodities and traded by other inmates (Sykes, 1958), which only serves to illustrate the lack of respect given to those who are not willing or able to exert their masculinity or dominance within the inmate subculture.

Fleisher and Krienert (2009) found similar sex role designations. The "homosexual persona" was categorized by "queens," "true homosexuals," and "punks" (p. 66). The "true homosexual" was more respected than the "punk," because the "true homosexual" did not change his behavior upon incarceration. On the other hand, "punks" were "turned out" and perceived to be weak because they caved under pressure (p. 67). The "queens" were similar to the "fags" identified by Hensley and colleagues (2003).

The Informal Economy

Because they are far removed from society, inmates lose access to the free market for goods and services. As a result of this deprivation, they often participate in their own informally structured, black market economy. Although this system includes goods, such as drugs, weapons, and cigarettes, it also includes services. These services sometimes include protection from violence or providing sexual favors.

One example of sexual favors being used as a bartering tool in the informal economy occurs in what Donaldson (2003) refers to as "protective pairing." Protective pairing is an agreement made between weaker inmates and stronger ones. Under these agreements, the weaker inmates receive protection from stronger inmates. In exchange, the weaker inmates perform duties that are viewed as more feminine in nature, such as housekeeping duties or sexual favors for their protector (Trammell, 2011). By examining the nature behind this type of consensual activity, we find that clearly much of the sexual activity that occurs that is thought to be consensual is really "pseudo-consensual" (Koscheski et al., 2002, p. 131). Inmates who engage in these activities often do so begrudgingly, as payment for services, or for protection against violence from stronger inmates. Thus, these inmates have been "turned out" (Fleisher and Krienert, 2009).

Overcrowding

The United States has the highest rate of incarceration in the world (Walmsley, 2009), with a correctional population of more than two million individuals (Glaze, 2010). Overcrowding is inarguably one of the leading contributors to prison violence, especially prison sexual violence (Gibbons, 2011; Hassine, 2010). However, the same factors contributing to forced sexual activity likely also lead to increases in consensual sexual activity among inmates.

For instance, cells originally designed for one inmate now house at least two, and sometimes as many as three or four inmates. In some facilities, gymnasiums and other large rooms have been converted into dormitory-style housing units. While the literature has found a clear and consistent link between sexual violence and crowding (Gibbons, 2011; Hagemann, 2008; Hassine, 2010; Wooldredge and Steiner, 2009), a logical assumption would also be that a link also exists between overcrowding and an increase in consensual sex as well. More inmates in confined spaces increase the opportunities for consensual sex. With the ratio of inmates to guards being quite high (Byrne and Hummer, 2008), detecting consensual sex becomes more difficult. This difficulty is especially true of activities occurring during the nighttime hours, when they can be easily concealed among cell mates.

Inmate Consensual Sex in Female Institutions

Consensual sexual relationships among females have historically been viewed dramatically differently than those occurring among males. While sexually violent acts have gained greater acceptance and become more tolerated by male inmates, consensual sex is often viewed as less acceptable (Belknap, 2007). In contrast, for females consensual sex is more likely to be viewed as acceptable (Belknap, 2007), and in many instances is considered seductive and womanly behavior (Banbury, 2004).

Female inmates typically have vastly different interpersonal relationships than their male counterparts. Whereas males are apt to have violent interactions with one another, often based on gang membership and a hierarchical structure, females are less likely to subscribe to this type of social environment. Similarly to males, they may become situationally homosexual or bisexual and may or may not maintain these identities upon their release from prison (Diaz-Cotto, 1996; Belknap, 2007). For decades, it has been well cited that female inmates often form pseudofamilies (Keys, 2002; Ward and Kassenbaum, 1965). This pseudofamily structure is quite common, with as many as 70 percent of female inmates belonging to a pseudofamily (MacKenzie, Robinson, and Campbell, 1989; Trammell, 2012).

Although females do not have a hierarchical structure that mimics that of male inmates, the pseudofamily environment allows them to divide the members between "butch" and "femme" inmates. Inmates considered "butch" are likely to be more dominant and hold control and power in the pseudofamily. "Femme" inmates may trade sexual favors for goods and services (Ward and Kassebaum, 1965). Pseudofamilies are patterned after typical family structures, often consisting of fathers, mothers, siblings, nephews, nieces, and cousins. More experienced and prisonized inmates take on parental roles over their "children," newer inmates who have yet to be fully immersed into the prison culture.

Indications can be found that the pseudofamily structure may be less prominent than before. As female inmates begin to have more readily accessible educational and vocational opportunities, their involvement in pseudofamilies may be decreasing (Fox, 1984). Some inmates fear that involvement in a pseudofamily may lead to increased scrutiny from correctional staff, and therefore they may be less likely to become members of one (Belknap, 2007). Moreover, some argue that the primary function of pseudofamilies is to provide emotional support, not sexual relationships (Huggins, Capeheart, and Newman, 2006), so that involvement in pseudofamilies may have little influence on the likelihood that a female inmate will be involved in consensual sexual relationships. Some criticize the early research on pseudofamilies as too simplistic and homophobic in nature (Belknap, 2007), providing little explanation or insight into the female inmate subculture. Newer studies have found women's sexuality in prison to be more fluid, accepted by inmates, and common among the female inmates prior to incarceration (Fleisher and Krienert, 2009).

Consensual Sex Between
Correctional Staff and Inmates

Sexual relations between correctional staff and inmates are strictly prohibited. In part, this prohibition results from the fact that these relationships can never be truly consensual due to the power differential between the two groups (Calhoun and Coleman, 2002) even if the encounter was initiated by the inmate (Worley and Cheeseman, 2006). Correctional officers hold a great deal of power over the inmates, and sexual relations can greatly upset this power. For instance, officers may give preferential treatment to inmates providing them with sexual favors. If these relationships are terminated, then the officers may revoke the inmates' privileges. Despite the explicit prohibition of sexual relations between staff and inmates, these incidents may not be punished as severely as coercive relationships (Owen and Moss, 2009).

Consensual sexual relationships have historically been a primary concern between the female inmate population and correctional staff

(Owen and Moss, 2009). In Fleisher and Krienert's (2009) study, 66 percent of male inmates and 71 percent of female inmates reported knowing about staff and inmate sexual relationships. However, recent surveys indicate this issue to be more frequently cited among male inmates. Of the inmates surveyed in 2008, 2.6 percent of females and 4.8 percent of males reported having consensual sexual relations with correctional staff (Beck and Johnson, 2012). By far, the greatest prevalence of these incidents occurred between female correctional officers and male inmates (86 percent), and only about 5.5 percent of the incidents were between male correctional officers and female inmates (Beck and Johnson, 2012).

Other studies support the finding that inappropriate sexual relationships are more likely among female correctional officers and male inmates. For example, Marquart, Barnhill, and Balshaw-Biddle (2001) examined the personnel records of 508 correctional officers for employee boundary violations and found that 12 percent were disciplined for sexual contact with inmates. Furthermore, female staff made up 60 percent of the violators during the four-year period examined. As Fleisher and Krienert (2009) noted, however, some of these relationships are formed on the basis of manipulation by the male inmate.

Correctional Staff Perceptions

Until relatively recently, sexual misconduct was an issue that received little attention. With the passage of the Prison Rape Elimination Act (PREA) in 2003, however, more focus began to be directed toward sexual victimization among inmates. As a result, correctional administrators have been directed to devote more resources, training, and education to dealing with prevention of sexual violence.

The issue of consensual sex seems to remain questionable. As recently as 2005, prison wardens were still indicating that consensual sex, as well as other forms of sexual activity, was not occurring frequently among the inmate population (Hensley and Tewksbury, 2005b). Despite the alleged consensual nature of the sexual activity, it is still prohibited, and correctional officers are expected to respond to these infractions just as they would any other form of rule violation. Many state institutions have adopted "zero-tolerance" policies on any form of sexual activity occurring between inmates, and between inmates and correctional staff (Thompson, Nored, and Dial, 2008).

Correctional officers and staff have difficulty discerning consensual sex from coercive or even violent sexual acts (Owen and Moss, 2009; Wooden and Parker, 1982). As much as 96 percent of correctional officers surveyed cannot easily distinguish between different types of sexual activity (Eigenberg, 2000). Unless an act is overtly violent, they may dismiss it as consensual. As Eigenberg (2000) observes, "some officers may fail to define some acts of rape simply because a knife is not at a man's throat during the sexual act" (p. 417).

Correctional officers may view all sexual activity occurring among the inmate population as being equally sordid. Prior research indicates that about half of the correctional officers surveyed indicated that if an inmate had previously been involved in consensual sex, then any sexual violence against them is seen as a deserved response (Eigenberg, 1989). Results such as this illustrate that correctional staff view consensual sex as an invitation for coercive or even abusive sexual activities. Their rationale remains unclear. Perhaps correctional officers view all sexual activities as participation in the prison subculture.

Even when an act is clearly identifiable as consensual, correctional staff may be less likely to respond to these incidents than either coercive or violent sexual activity (Owen and Moss, 2009). If they happen upon two men having consensual sex, they may simply feel too embarrassed to intervene (Eigenberg, 2000). They may feel the behavior is occurring among consenting adults and is not harmful to either party. Moreover, much of the knowledge correctional officers have with inmate sexual activity may not be from direct exposure. They were more likely to obtain their knowledge either from reading official reports or from discussions with other correctional officers (Owen and Wells, 2006). Therefore, they may lack the familiarity with incidents involving the wide spectrum of sexual relations among prisoners.

Correctional administrators are also highly unlikely to want the negative publicity associated with any form of sexual activity, regardless of whether it is consensual or not. As the public becomes more aware of the negative impact of sexual activity among inmates, in part due to the passage of PREA (Corlew, 2006), the quest for in-

stitutional accountability will likely increase. In order to prevent negative reactions from the public, issues concerning consensual sex will
more probably be tolerated and not be officially reported or documented (Hensley, Tewksbury, and Wright, 2001).

Finally, many of the norms and values of the prison subculture
are tolerated by prison staff. For instance, prison violence, including
gang violence, may be overlooked by correctional authorities because it acts as a potential means of exerting informal social control
among the inmate population (Gilligan, 2002). Consensual sexual activity may simply be one more tolerated behavior in an attempt to
allow inmates to exert control over one another (Hensley, Tewksbury,
and Wright, 2001).

In sum, a wide range of attitudes and perceptions are presented
by correctional staff with respect to consensual sex among inmates.
As Donaldson (1993b) indicates, "consensual activities are accepted
as inevitable by some, hunted out and seriously punished when discovered by others, while most tend to look the other way so long as
the behavior does not become disruptive or too open" (p. 348).

Policies and Solutions for Consensual Sex

Regardless of the institutional rules and regulations, consensual sex
is likely to continue to occur. Because much of the explanation for
consensual sex is based on a lack of heterosexual opportunities, few
options seem to exist from an administration standpoint to completely prevent sexual activity. Some policy avenues that should be
explored include cocorrectional facilities, providing condoms to inmates, and allowing for conjugal visits (discussed more extensively
in Chapter 5).

Cocorrectional Facilities

Historically, correctional facilities all housed both male and female
inmates, with females being segregated to a separate wing or floor of
the institution. The modern version of cocorrectional institutions
began in the 1970s with two facilities, one in Massachusetts and one
in Texas. In the United States, currently ninety-three state and federal
institutions are considered cocorrectional (Stinchcomb, 2011).

In addition to providing equitable programming opportunities and being more cost effective, cocorrectional facilities could potentially reduce sexual activities among inmates. Although sex is prohibited, no one can assume that it will not occur. Moreover, the belief is that by housing both male and female inmates in the same institution, even though not in the same cells, a disruption would occur in the masculine ideals of the prison environment, making much of the existing situational homosexual sex unnecessary. In these facilities, "men are not pressured to portray the hardened, macho image required to avoid appearing weak in a male institution. They tend to behave better in the presence of women and engage in fewer fights, since proving one's toughness does not become the 'badge of honor' that it is in male institutions" (Stinchcomb, 2011, p. 147).

Despite this belief, studies indicate that these institutions are unlikely to decrease the rates of homosexual activity (Campbell, 1980; Ross and Fabiano, 1986, as cited in Belknap, 2007). Cocorrectional facilities seem particularly detrimental to female inmates. The prevalence of both pregnancy and prostitution increases (Chesney-Lind and Rodriguez, 1983, as cited in Belknap, 2007; Hefferman and Krippel, 1980; Ruback, 1980). Women are also likely to fulfill the more subservient roles in the prison hierarchy (Belknap, 2007), those which would formerly have been adopted by the weaker male inmates.

Condoms

Although condoms will not prevent consensual sex, their availability can greatly reduce the spread of sexually transmitted diseases. Less than 1 percent of prisons currently distribute condoms or make them readily available to inmates (McClure, 2008). A great deal of resistance has arisen to providing condoms to inmates. Less than 20 percent of correctional staff surveyed believed condoms should be available to inmates (Tewksbury and Mustaine, 2005). Given the spontaneous and violent nature of sexual assault, inmates will be unlikely to use condoms in instances of forced sexual intercourse. Condoms also have the possibility to be used as weapons, either by filling them with dirt or by using them as strangulation devices (Nerenberg, 2002). Another concern is that providing condoms might imply that the correctional institution permits sexual activity (Blumberg and Laster, 2009).

Regardless of whether condoms are available, inmates will clearly likely continue to engage in sexual activity. Much of the condom debate seems to focus on violent sexual acts. Recent research has shown promising results. After condoms were introduced in prisons in New South Wales, Australia, a decrease actually occurred in both sexual violence and consensual sex. Moreover, between 1996 and 2005, only three incidents of condoms being used as weapons against correctional officers were reported, all of which were not considered serious (Yap et al., 2007). Installation of condom machines in a jail has also resulted in positive outcomes. Despite prior concerns, sexual activity among inmates did not increase. The easy accessibility of having condoms dispensed from a machine also seems to have made a difference. Prisoners' awareness of access to condoms increased, and condom usage, especially among high-risk individuals, also increased (Sylla, Harawa, and Reznick, 2010).

Conclusion

The very nature of consensual sex, as illustrated in the discussion throughout this chapter, is complex. Correctional administrators struggle with the identification and sanctioning of consensual sex, an issue that is further exacerbated by a lack of a consistent definition. Furthermore, due to the single-gender nature of correctional institutions and the unique nature of the inmate subculture, successful identification and sanctioning of it would likely do little to prevent sexual activities from occurring.

3

Sexual Victimization

Richard Tewksbury and David P. Connor

In recent years, sexual victimization among individuals housed in US correctional institutions has received increased attention. Specifically, with the passage of the Prison Rape Elimination Act of 2003, the subject of sexual violence behind bars has aroused significant interest among citizens, correctional practitioners, and criminal justice scholars alike. As discussed in this chapter, scientific knowledge about this phenomenon is derived from numerous research endeavors. Investigations into prison sexual victimization are fairly extensive; at the same time, in regard to certain issues, such studies are also relatively limited. What is available, however, provides a baseline of understanding concerning the incidence and prevalence of sexual violence in correctional settings, characteristics of both victims and perpetrators, prison staff member perspectives on sexual victimization, the challenges of reporting, investigating, and prosecuting prison sexual violence, and the impact that prison sexual victimization may have on recidivism.

Early Prison Sexual Victimization Research (1940–1989)

Early research on prison sexual victimization afforded scholars and practitioners a range of incident rates and patterns of nonconsensual sex. The variability of sexual assault measurements in these studies is rather striking. Despite research spanning nearly fifty years, researchers could not illustrate the problematic nature of prison sexual violence with precision.

Early studies described both the prevalence of prison sexual assault among inmates and the dynamics of such incidents. In one of the early, classic studies of life in prison, Clemmer (1940) noted that sex in prison had almost always been present, and the culture of the prison environment likely facilitated sexual activity between inmates. From his sample, Clemmer approximated that the prison population consisted of "normal" (60 percent), "quasi-normal" (30 percent), and "abnormal" (10 percent) inmates (p. 257). Although normal inmates refrained from involvement in sexual activity, "quasi-normal" (i.e., "wolves," "jockers," or "daddies") and "abnormal" (i.e., "inverts" or "sexual psychopaths") inmates commonly participated in sex behind bars.

The first widely cited, valid, and reliable incidence rate of inmate sexual victimization, however, was not available until 1968. In his study, Davis (1968) contended that 2,000 male inmates were sexually assaulted over a twenty-six-month period, while in the custody of Philadelphia jail officials. Drawing on interviews with more than 3,300 inmates and 570 staff members, as well as reviews of institutional records, he initially documented 156 incidents of rape. Based on this statistic from his sample, Davis then estimated a total number of sexual victimization incidents for the more than 60,000 inmates that passed through the jail system. He concluded that the total number was close to 2,000 sexual assaults.

Following the work of Davis (1968), little attention was devoted to the issue of sexual violence in correctional settings for more than a decade. Disrupting this paucity of research, Nacci (1978) focused on the dynamics of sexual assault inside federal prisons, utilizing self-report data from 330 randomly selected male inmates housed in seventeen different federal prisons. Twelve percent (n = 40) of the inmates reported that they had participated in sexual contact at their current prison, and less than 1 percent (n = 2) reported that they had been victims of nonconsensual sex. From this study, prison sexual victimization appeared to be far less commonplace than either Davis's estimate or Nacci's own finding of the rate of consensual sexual behavior between male inmates.

Distinguishing between institutional and community sexual assault against males, Groth (1979) sampled twenty perpetrators and seven victims involved in prison sexual assault. All of the inmates committing sexual assault in prison reported that they had either penetrated another inmate or forced another inmate to perform oral sex. The most noticeable feature of institutionalized male rape, according to Groth, was the fact that 80 percent of the prison sexual assaults were "gang rapes," compared to 32 percent of community sexual assaults.

Moss, Hosford, and Anderson, also in 1979, reported that, in a one-year period, only 1 percent (n = 12) from a sample of 1,100 inmates housed in a federal correctional institution were recognized by correctional officers as perpetrators of sexual assault. Of those inmates who were identified by prison staff members as perpetrators, seven were black, and five were Chicano. Almost without exception, white inmates were identified by prison staff members as victims. In fact, only two inmates described as sexual assault victims were not white. Most importantly, in each documented case of sexual violence, the researchers found that identified perpetrators and victims were of different races, which caused them to conclude that the "racial composition of assaulters and victims" may be more problematic than the actual incidence rate of sexual assault (p. 823). Similarly, Carroll (1977) observed the "biracial character of sexual assaults," believing that racial hostility generated an underlying motivation for prison sexual victimization (pp. 418–419). The interracial nature of prison sex assault was one of the most strongly established "facts" of early prison sex research.

The study of prison sexual violence was significantly advanced, with a focus on more than simply documentation and racial characteristics of victims and perpetrators, with the publication of Lockwood's *Prison Sexual Violence* (1980). Drawing on data from a sample of male inmates, Lockwood studied institutional violence inside the New York State prison system. Following interviews with seventy-four inmates from two different correctional institutions, Lockwood reported that 28 percent claimed that they had been targets of sexual perpetrators in prison. However, only one inmate reported that he had been a victim of a completed sexual assault. These inmates also described fifty-one total incidents of sexual assault or other physical violence, and they detailed ninety-seven incidents of less aggressive sexual behavior. Nearly one-half of the described violent incidents involved high levels of force, such as sexual assault, stabbing, clubbing, or beating. Essentially, inmates were relatively obliging in their disclosure of violent victimizations, but they were more reluctant in describing sexual victimizations. By the same token, Bowker (1980) asserted that violence was often both customary behind bars and perpetrated by older inmates who extended protection to younger inmates in exchange for sex. Both researchers (Bowker, 1980; Lockwood, 1980) concluded that the driving force behind all types of prison violence could be explained by the motivations to obtain desired rewards (i.e., instrumental violence) or the desire to express a position of strength to other inmates (i.e., expressive violence).

More recent research addressing the existence and incidence of prison sexual violence continued to show a range of victimization rates, which largely varied by types of samples and approaches to collecting data. Showing one of the highest rates of sexual victimization, Wooden and Parker's (1982) study in one medium security prison suggested that prison rape was relatively common among male inmates. They surveyed 200 inmates housed in California, and they reported that 14 percent of these individuals had been sexually victimized during their incarceration. Fifty-two percent of the inmates who participated in the study reported that they had been coerced into sexual activity. Perhaps the most disturbing finding was the report that inmates were forced into long-term sexual victimization patterns, including protective pairings (i.e., "partnering" with another inmate in a sexual relationship in exchange for protection). Beyond their surveys, Wooden and Parker also interviewed eighty inmates who identified themselves as homosexuals, and 40 percent of these individuals reported that they had been forced to engage in sex during their present incarceration.

At about the same time, similar rates of victimization were reported for a stratified sample of inmates housed in seventeen federal prisons (Nacci and Kane, 1983, 1984a, 1984b). Inside the Federal Bureau of Prisons, Nacci and Kane (1983, 1984a, 1984b) conducted interviews with both inmates and correctional officers. Twelve percent of the 330 inmates who participated in this study reported that they had participated in at least one homosexual act during their present incarceration. Most notably, 29 percent of the inmates who participated in the study reported that they had been propositioned for sex, and 7 percent reported that they had been coerced into sexual activity. However, less than 1 percent of the inmates reported that they had been forced to perform sexual acts, and less than 1 percent reported that they had been raped.

Following the publication of Wooden and Parker's (1982) and Nacci and Kane's (1983, 1984a, 1984b) research, inquiries into prison sexual violence largely went into abeyance for the better part of a decade. Reflecting on this period, Tewksbury and West (2000) concluded that, while a handful of scholars addressed both consensual sex and the presence of HIV/AIDS in correctional facilities, attention to sexual violence in prisons and jails was scant. They also contended that sexual victimization in prison, when addressed in research, was only corollary to other studies. In many ways, throughout the 1980s, concerns about sexual victimization of inmates waned, research efforts focused on other prison issues, and scholars, practitioners, and the public more or less acknowledged that they understood how common sexual assault was in prison. Sexual violence in correctional institutions was not a large enough issue to merit serious, ongoing attention.

The next research to appear, however, was both important and came in a wave of studies. This wave was contained in a book and a two-volume, special issue of *The Prison Journal,* with four articles addressing prison sexual violence. Surveying 150 Ohio inmates, Tewksbury's (1989a) study centered on inmate reports of sexual assaults, forceful sexual strategies, and sexual propositions offered by inmates. Interestingly, none of the inmates who participated in the study reported that they had been sexually assaulted or raped. However, 14 percent of the inmates reported that they had been approached for sex with force.

Both Smith and Batiuk (1989) and Jones and Schmid (1989) focused on identifying how inmates managed self-presentations in order to avoid sexual victimization. However, neither of these studies addressed measures of incidence or prevalence of sexual violence in prison, instead taking the existence of such as a given. Also utilizing qualitative methodology, Chonco (1989) drew on interviews with forty inmates in a midwestern prerelease correctional facility to examine inmates' conceptions of what made them more or less likely to be sexually victimized while in prison. Unfortunately, he also did not provide any measurements or estimates of incidence or prevalence. Likewise, Fleisher (1989) chose to investigate the roles and inter-action strategies that inmates used to avoid sexual violence, rather than the frequency of such victimization, in his ethnographic study of the US Penitentiary in Lompoc, California.

Prison Sexual Victimization Research (1990–2005)

The topic of prison sexual victimization was next revisited in the re-search literature, and in a way that emphasized identifying frequency, by Saum and colleagues' (1995) survey of 101 Delaware inmates. Twelve percent of the inmates in the study reported that they had wit-nessed a rape occur in the correctional institution, and 40 percent claimed to have personally known about a rape in the previous year. However, only one inmate self-reported a completed rape, and only five inmates reported that another inmate had attempted to sexually assault them. Still, almost 39 percent of the inmates believed that rapes happened once a week or more, and almost 16 percent felt that sexual assaults were a daily occurrence. Such data suggest the need to question why a large discrepancy exists between actual and per-ceived sexual assault in prison.

In 1996, Maitland and Sluder (see also Maitland and Sluder, 1998) released a study that summarized a variety of victimization forms experienced and reported by inmates housed in one midwest-ern prison. Relying on surveys from a nonrandom sample, they re-ported that almost 1 percent of the inmates indicated that they had been a victim of forced sexual activity, and 16 percent indicated that they had been recipients of unwanted sexual comments. At the same time, research by Struckman-Johnson and colleagues began to pro-vide a series of studies that represented the next significant works ad-dressing prison sexual violence. However, these studies produced very different results from those of other scholars in the preceding decade. In the first study (Struckman-Johnson et al., 1996), 22 percent of the male inmates were identified through self-reports as victims of sexual coercion, and one-quarter of these incidents were identified as "gang rapes." Following up on these results, Struckman-Johnson and Struckman-Johnson (2000) used anonymous surveys collected from 1,799 inmates and 475 staff members living and working in seven correctional institutions throughout four midwestern jurisdictions. This follow-up study produced very similar results to the original 1996 study, with 21 percent of the male inmates reporting at least one instance of forced or pressured sexual contact, and 7 percent reporting that they had been raped during their incarceration. Perhaps most importantly, the 2000 study was distinguished from previous efforts, as it also addressed staff sexual misconduct. One in five inmates reported sexual coercion or assault perpetrated by a staff member.

However, not all research of this era reported such high rates of sexual victimization. Hensley, Tewksbury, and Castle (2003) reported that only 1 percent of a sample of male inmates incarcerated in Oklahoma were sexual violence victims. However, 14 percent reported that they had been threatened or targets of attempted sexual coercion. Using survey data from 142 inmates in one maximum security prison, Hensley, Koscheski, and Tewksbury (2005) asserted that more than 8 percent of the inmates had been sexually victimized while incarcerated. And, employing a very different approach, Human Rights Watch's (2001) three-year study of more than 200 inmates, as well as surveys with state correctional system officials across the United States, produced a report entitled *No Escape: Male Rape in U.S. Prisons*. The primary conclusion of Human Rights Watch's investigation, which drew on numerous firsthand, detailed accounts of rape and sexual coercion, was that sexual abuse clearly took place in US prisons housing male inmates. While documenting the occurrence of prison sexual victimization, the nature of the research failed to produce a statistical rate of incidence or prevalence. The data, however, provided a strong argument that sexual violence did occur in US prisons and jails at rates unacknowledged by correctional officials. According to the study, "the hard facts about inmate-on-inmate sexual abuse are little known," and conclusive national data regarding such sexual victimization did not exist (Human Rights Watch, 2001, p. 1).

Contemporary Prison Sexual Victimization Research (2006–Present)

Following the passage of the Prison Rape Elimination Act (PREA), studies examining prison sexual victimization have become more plentiful, and research methodologies have also been improved in the

arena of prison sexual violence. Much of this new era of research has
been a direct outgrowth of PREA, with most of this work completed,
in one way or another, with PREA funds. One significant piece of research that appeared in the post-PREA era was the JFA Institute's
National Institute of Justice–funded study of sexual violence in Texas
prisons (Austin et al., 2006). This review of more than three years of
data from the nation's largest prison system showed that only about 2
percent of the daily population of Texas prisons were classified as a
perpetrator or victim. Over the course of three years and eight
months, a total of 1,938 allegations of sexual assault were reported.
However, according to Texas Department of Criminal Justice officials, only forty-three (i.e., about 2 percent) of the allegations were
sustained after investigation.

    In one of the most methodologically sophisticated studies to
date, Wolff and colleagues (2006) were funded by the Bureau of Justice Assistance to use audio computer-assisted self-interview technology to conduct anonymous self-report surveys with inmates in one
mid-Atlantic state in 2006. In this study, sexual victimization was
measured in two ways. First, the researchers used a single-item,
"global" measure of victimization (which had been the standard in
research up to this date), and second, they used a ten-item, behavior-
specific scale that incorporated both staff and inmate perpetrated sexual violence. Across their entire period of incarceration, nearly 2 percent of male inmates and nearly 4 percent of female inmates reported
that they had been sexually victimized by another inmate. Significantly higher rates of victimization were reported for staff-perpetrated
sexual victimization, with more than 5 percent of male inmates and
more than 3 percent of female inmates responding that they had been
sexually victimized by a prison staff member. In addition to measur-
ing victimization across the entire period of incarceration, the authors
of this study also asked inmates about sexual victimization during the
previous six months. Results showed that measurements using the
ten-item, behavior-specific approach yielded rates that were two to
nine times higher than results using a single-item, global measure.
The results from the ten-item, behavior-specific measure showed that
nearly 4 percent of male inmates had been sexually victimized by another inmate, and nearly 7 percent had been sexually victimized by
a prison staff member in the previous six months. Among female
inmates, 21 percent reported that they had been sexually victimized

by another inmate, and nearly 8 percent reported that they had been sexually victimized by a prison staff member. Here, we must point out that the very high rate of inmate-perpetrated victimization reported by female inmates was primarily due to a high rate of abusive sexual contacts (i.e., the "lesser" form of sexual violence included in today's standard definitions of prison sexual violence).

Other post-PREA research has not drawn on government funding, but such studies have provided important insights concerning prison sexual victimization. Struckman-Johnson and Struckman-Johnson (2006) surveyed 1,788 inmates in ten midwestern prisons. The researchers used a single-item, global measure of sexual assault (i.e., "Have you been forced or pressured to have sexual contact at this prison?"), and they found that 21 percent of the male inmates and 19 percent of the female inmates reported experiencing sexual victimization.

The National Former Prisoner Survey was conducted between January 2008 and October 2008 by the Bureau of Justice Statistics, with assistance from the National Opinion Research Center at the University of Chicago. From 317 randomly selected parole offices in forty states, 18,526 former state inmates under active parole supervision were randomly selected to participate in the survey (Beck and Johnson, 2012). More than 11 percent of the former inmates reported that they had experienced one or more incidents of sexual victimization during the most recent period of incarceration. Using weights to produce national-level estimates, the projected number of former state inmates who experienced prison sexual victimization totaled nearly 10 percent of all former state inmates under active parole supervision at mid-year 2008. Among all former state inmates, nearly 2 percent reported that they had experienced one or more incidents while housed in a local jail, nearly 8 percent while housed in a state prison, and less than 1 percent while housed in a community treatment facility.

The largest and most methodologically sophisticated study of prison sexual violence is the PREA-mandated National Inmate Survey, which is conducted by the Bureau of Justice Statistics. Drawing on data collected via audio computer-assisted self-interview technology from a stratified random sample of inmates in all fifty states, the Bureau of Justice Statistics provided the most rigorous assessments of the incidence and prevalence of prison sexual violence ever. While collecting their data from inmates, the Bureau of Justice Statistics also collected data on the number of sexual violence incidents reported by inmates to correctional officials.

In the report on incidents in 2004 (Beck and Harrison, 2005), more than 8,200 incidents of sexual violence were officially reported to adult and juvenile correctional authorities, with one-quarter of these events being subsequently substantiated by correctional investigations. Rates were highest in both state-operated and private juvenile facilities, and rates were lowest in state prisons for adults. Of all allegations reported by correctional authorities, 41 percent involved staff-on-inmate sexual misconduct, 37 percent involved inmate-on-inmate nonconsensual sexual acts (e.g., acts involving penetration), 10 percent involved inmate-on-inmate abusive sexual contacts (e.g. nonpenetrative acts, such as fondling), and 11 percent involved staff sexual harassment of inmates. In 2005, a total of 6,241 allegations were reported in adult prisons and jails. The 2005 rate represents a slight increase in the rate of allegations from 2004 (i.e., 2.8 per 1,000 inmates in 2005, compared to 2.5 per 1,000 inmates in 2004). As in 2004, the most common types of allegations involved staff sexual misconduct with inmates (38 percent), followed by inmate-on-inmate nonconsensual sexual acts (35 percent), staff sexual harassment of inmates (17 percent), and inmate-on-inmate abusive sexual contacts (10 percent).

In 2007, the first National Inmate Survey (Beck and Harrison, 2007a, 2008) was conducted, and the second National Inmate Survey (Beck and Harrison, 2010) was conducted between October 2008 and December 2009. The second National Inmate Survey (Beck and Harrison, 2010) sampled inmates housed in 167 state and federal prisons and 286 local jails. The survey also included inmates housed in ten institutions operated by Immigration and Customs Enforcement, Indian tribes, and the US military. Ultimately, 81,566 inmates participated in the survey, including 32,029 prison inmates, 48,066 jail inmates, 957 Immigration and Customs Enforcement inmates, 399 military inmates, and 115 Indian tribe inmates.

Interestingly, rates of sexual victimization among inmates remained largely the same between the first and second National Inmate Survey. More than 4 percent of the prison inmates and more than 3 percent of the jail inmates, in both the first (Beck and Harrison, 2007b, 2008) and second National Inmate Survey (Beck and Harrison, 2010), reported that they had experienced one or more incidents of sexual victimization by another inmate or staff member in the past twelve months or since admission to the correctional facility (if less than twelve months).

In May 2012, data collection was completed for the third National Inmate Survey. Notably, this third research endeavor by the Bureau of Justice Statistics modified the previous survey design. The new survey included measures of mental health, physical health, facility safety, and facility security. This modification also allowed the survey to obtain the first national-level estimates of sexual victimization among inmates under age eighteen.

In addition to documenting the occurrence and characteristics of inmates involved in prison sexual violence, the post-PREA era has also seen an expansion of research foci into the consequences of such actions. One of the least addressed areas of research related to prison sexual violence is the question of if and how sexual victimization while incarcerated may or may not have an effect on subsequent criminality (and other forms of behavior). To date, only two studies (Heil et al., 2009; Listwan and Hanley, 2012) have addressed these issues. Heil and colleagues (2009) tracked groups of offenders, including inmates known to have committed sexual offenses while incarcerated, for five years after release from prison. They concluded that recidivism rates for offenders who committed sexual offenses while incarcerated were higher than the recidivism rates for offenders who did not commit sexual offenses while incarcerated. Also, the recidivism offenses of these offenders were more likely than the offenses of other offenders to involve a sexual component. Specifically, nearly 53 percent of offenders who committed a sexual offense while incarcerated were reincarcerated, and 87 percent of such offenders were rearrested within five years of release. Finally, Heil and colleagues also showed that offenders who committed sexual offenses while incarcerated not only recidivated at a higher rate than offenders who did not commit a sexual offense while incarcerated, but also recidivated in shorter periods of time (i.e., an average of 812 versus 909 days to a new sexual offense arrest and 389 versus 491 days to any new arrest). In summary, Heil and colleagues concluded that sexual offending in prison was a significant risk indicator for new sexual, violent, and other arrests in the community.

By examining the outcomes among 1,600 formerly incarcerated offenders who served time in Ohio halfway houses, Listwan and Hanley (2012) attempted to measure the impact of prison sexual victimization on the process of reentering society. Halfway house residents were followed in the community for an average of two and one-half years, and face-to-face interviews were conducted with the residents. Nearly 20 percent indicated that they had witnessed sexual coercion during their previous incarceration, and 12 percent indicated that they had seen a rape. Five percent indicated that someone had attempted to coerce them into sex, and 1 percent indicated that they had been the victim of an attempted rape. One percent reported that they had been the victim of sexual coercion or rape during their previous incarceration.

Most importantly, in Listwan and Hanley's (2012) study, 48 percent of the sample were arrested (17 percent for a violent offense), and 41 percent were returned to prison. The multivariate analysis of arrest showed that witnessing prison sexual victimization was a significant predictor of arrest in the community. Those who were younger, had a greater number of prior felony convictions, had a violent history, were not employed in the community, participated in treatment in the community, and experienced direct violent victimization in prison were more likely to be returned to prison during the follow-up period.

In sum, research efforts focusing on the numerous issues related to prison sexual victimization have greatly increased in recent years, and the quality of data and findings have also improved substantially. A problem that was previously given virtually no scholarly or research attention is now being examined from a variety of perspectives. PREA significantly aided researchers, correctional systems, staff members, and inmates who experienced prison sexual violence through the dedication of funds to solving a problem that still needs significant scholarly inquiry. This increased research focus is anticipated to continue to permit progress in the plight against sexual victimization in US prisons.

Research on Female Inmates

At one time, research focused on documenting and identifying rates of sexual violence among incarcerated women was extremely rare. Not until the 1990s was serious scholarly attention devoted to the issue of sexual victimization of female inmates. The first study to use true social science methods was Struckman-Johnson and colleagues, in 1996. In this study, which drew on data from ninety-three females incarcerated in one midwestern prison, the researchers reported a 7 percent rate of sexual victimization, compared to a 22 percent rate of sexual victimization for males across six facilities. Struckman-Johnson and Struckman-Johnson (2002) also reported on data collected from 1,263 female inmates in three prisons, and they showed a wide range of victimization rates. In one facility, 19 percent of female inmates reported that they had been victims of sexual abuse in their present facility, and 27 percent reported that they had been victims of sexual abuse at some point during their incarceration. However, in two much smaller prisons, victimization rates were only 8 percent and 6 percent, respectively. Across all three prisons, the most commonly reported incident was sexual fondling, although descriptions of one in five incidents constituted rape.

Using a different approach, Alarid (2000a) described the incidence of, and issues related to, sexual assault and sexual coercion among incarcerated women by conducting a content analysis of one female inmate's prison letters over a five-year period. Similar to the studies of sexual assault and coercion in male prisons, she discovered that many incidents of sexual victimization were unreported and that official reports necessarily represented a significant underreporting for sexual assaults in female correctional institutions. In contrast to the official statistics, Alarid (2000a) contended that some female inmates were targets of sexual coercion on a daily basis. In discussing the occurrence of rape at the prison over the five-year period covered by her qualitative data, she concluded that "rape occurred at a much lower rate than other forms of sexual behavior. However, when rapes did occur among women offenders, there were multiple perpetrators rather than a single female offender" (p. 399).

Hensley, Castle, and Tewksbury (2003) surveyed 245 women in one southern prison, and they reported that 5 percent of these female inmates claimed to be victims of sexual coercion. Among incarcerated women, surveys with Australian inmates generated a rate of only 1 percent (Butler and Milner, 2003). And, although no generalizable rates of incidence or prevalence were produced, Stop Prisoner Rape (2003) investigated the Ohio Reformatory for Women and concluded that sexual abuse did occur in the institution and that administrative attitudes, physical plant design, and "an environment consistently conducive to sexual abuse" all contributed to sexual violence against female inmates (p. 16).

According to data on sexual violence reported to correctional officials, female jail inmates may be especially vulnerable to staff sexual misconduct. Calhoun and Coleman (2002) conducted focus
groups in a Hawaii prison for women, and they reported that inmates
estimated that 20 percent of the correctional officers at the correctional institution engaged in some form of sexual activity with female inmates. Consistent with official records of reported sexual violence, 78 percent of staff sexual misconduct allegations in jails
involved female inmates. In contrast, only 33 percent of staff sexual
misconduct in prisons involved female inmates. However, women
constituted only 14 percent of all prison and jail inmates at mid-year
2005 (Harrison and Beck, 2006), suggesting that female inmates are
overrepresented among sexually victimized inmates.

Owen and colleagues (2008) utilized focus groups with female
inmates. A total of forty focus groups, from two state prison systems
and three local jail systems, with 161 inmate and staff member participants, were conducted by the researchers. Analysis of focus group
data revealed that the "dynamic interplay between individual, rela-
tional, community, facility, and society factors create and sustain violence potentials in women's jails and prisons" (p. vi). In regard to
sexual violence specifically, such activity was rarely discussed by female inmates. However, when it was considered, sexual violence was
viewed as a product of problematic interpersonal relationships. The
most prevalent form of staff sexual misconduct described by female
inmates was inappropriate touching, comments and suggestions, or
other nonphysical assaults.

Most recently, data from the second National Inmate Survey
(Beck and Harrison, 2010) indicated that female inmates in prison
(4.7 percent) or jail (3.1 percent) were more than twice as likely as
male inmates in prison (1.9 percent) or jail (1.3 percent) to report that
they had experienced inmate-on-inmate sexual victimization. Among
inmates who reported inmate-on-inmate sexual victimization, only 4
percent of female inmates in prison and jail reported that they were
victimized within the first twenty-four hours after admission, compared to 13 percent of male prison inmates and 19 percent of male
jail inmates. Sexual activity with prison and jail staff members was
reported by 2.1 percent of female prison inmates and 1.5 percent of
female jail inmates, compared to 2.9 percent of male prison inmates
and 2.1 percent of male jail inmates. Among inmates who reported

staff-on-inmate sexual victimization, 5 percent of female prison inmates and 4 percent of female jail inmates reported that they were victimized within the first twenty-four hours after admission, compared to nearly 16 percent of male prison inmates and 30 percent of male jail inmates.

While research on sexual violence involving female inmates is still somewhat minimal, available studies suggest that this problem is not exclusively experienced by their male counterparts. Female inmates appear to experience sexual violence throughout the correctional system, with reported victimizations coming from both other inmates and staff. Future research, however, is needed to address issues unique to female inmates and the impact that prison violence has on such individuals.

Research on Victim Characteristics

When researchers have turned their attention to identifying characteristics of known or likely victims of prison sexual violence, a nearly exclusive focus has been given to adult males. As with many aspects of the prison rape issue, attention to women and juveniles is very rare. What is discussed below concerns adult male inmates, unless otherwise noted.

A number of factors have been identified by both researchers and advocacy groups as correlated with increased risk of sexual victimization during incarceration. For the most part, these findings are consistent across studies and advocates. Most attention to the issue of what places an inmate at increased risk for sexual victimization centers on demographics. Among the most well-established findings, both age and race appear to be critical factors in predicting an inmate's risk for sexual victimization. In regard to age, younger inmates are generally at greater risk. Most research (Austin et al., 2006; Hensley, Koscheski, and Tewksbury, 2005; Struckman-Johnson and Struckman-Johnson, 2006; Tewksbury, 1989a, 1989b) has suggested that inmates between approximately age twenty-nine and thirty-four are the most frequent victims of sexual victimization.

Austin and colleagues (2006) reported that, in Texas, the average age of victims in cases substantiated by officials is three years younger than the perpetrators. Others, however, have suggested that inmates at the very youngest end of the age continuum in adult prisons are at especially high risk of victimization (e.g., Listwan and Hanley, 2012). Across incidents substantiated by correctional officials, almost 53 percent of victims are under the age of twenty-five (Beck and Harrison, 2006). After controlling for multiple inmate characteristics, the second National Inmate Survey found that rates of reported staff sexual misconduct were lower among inmates ages twenty-five or older, compared to inmates ages twenty to twenty-four (Beck and Harrison, 2010).

A second well-established factor related to prison sexual victimization is race. Nationally, rates of inmate-on-inmate sexual victimization are higher among white prison inmates (3.0 percent), compared to black inmates (1.3 percent) (Beck and Harrison, 2010). Even in Texas, with only 31 percent of all the inmates classified as white (Texas Department of Criminal Justice, 2006), such "inmates are attacked more frequently than any other race. . . . Nearly 60% of sustained incidents involved a White victim, with 42% coming from Black assailants, and 9% coming from White assailants, followed by 7% from Hispanic assailants" (Austin et al., 2006). Similar results are also reported by researchers who relied on inmate self-reports. Wolff and colleagues (2006) reported that black inmates had the lowest rates of inmate-on-inmate sexual victimization (3.8 percent versus 4.9 percent for whites and 4.8 percent for Hispanics). However, for staff-on-inmate sexual victimizations, white inmates had the lowest rate (4.6 percent) versus 7.6 percent for Hispanic inmates, and 8.1 percent for black inmates. Struckman-Johnson and Struckman-Johnson (2006) similarly reported that 67 percent of self-identified male sexual assault victims in seven midwestern prisons were white; however, only 44 percent of self-identified female sexual assault victims were white. Hensley, Koscheski, and Tewksbury (2005) reported that in three Oklahoma prisons (i.e., one maximum, one medium, and one minimum security institution) fully 58 percent of self-identified sexual assault targets were white, compared to only 44 percent of the inmates housed in the three facilities. In addition, multivariate analysis in Listwan and Hanley's (2012) study showed that white inmates were more likely to report involvement in a violent victimization (including sexual violence).

Mentally ill or intellectually impaired inmates also appear to be at especially high risk of sexual assault. In Texas, Austin and colleagues (2006) reported that 12 percent of allegations of sexual assault involved such a victim. However, this population constituted only 1.6 percent of the incarcerated population. Another study suggested that inmates diagnosed with a mental illness were more likely to report involvement in a violent victimization, including sexual violence (Listwan and Hanley, 2012). Likewise, Wolff, Blitz, and Shi (2007) found that approximately one in twelve male inmates with a mental disorder reported at least one incident of sexual victimization by another inmate over a six-month period, compared to one in thirty-three male inmates without a mental disorder. Conversely, evidence also suggests that inmates with advanced educations may also be at greater risk for victimization. Struckman-Johnson and Struckman-Johnson (2006) reported that 40 percent of male victims and 51 percent of female victims had at least some college education. Nationally, rates of inmate-on-inmate sexual victimization among prison inmates were higher among inmates with a college degree (3.4 percent), compared to inmates who had not completed high school (2.0 percent) (Beck and Harrison, 2010).

In regard to criminal backgrounds, victims of sexual violence during incarceration are most likely to be serving a sentence for either a sexual offense or a nonviolent offense (Austin et al., 2006). Hensley and colleagues (2003) reported that targets of sexual coercion most often were incarcerated for an index offense conviction other than forcible rape (i.e., homicide, robbery, aggravated assault, burglary, larceny, motor vehicle theft, and arson). Nationally, though, inmates incarcerated for a violent sex offense indicate higher rates of inmate-on-inmate sexual victimization than inmates incarcerated for other offenses (Beck and Harrison, 2010).

Struckman-Johnson and Struckman-Johnson (2006) showed that inmates who identify as gay or bisexual were overrepresented among prison sexual violence victims. In their study, 11 percent of male respondents identified as gay or bisexual, whereas 25 percent of the victims identified as gay or bisexual. Among female inmates, 28 percent of the sample identified as gay or bisexual, whereas 36 percent of the victims identified as gay or lesbian. Similarly, Hensley, Koscheski, and Tewksbury (2005) reported that, in a southern maximum security facility, self-identified gay and bisexual inmates constituted 20 percent of the population, but accounted for 50 percent of the targets of sexual assaults. Nationally, an estimated 1.3 percent of heterosexual state and federal inmates reported that they had been sexually victimized by another inmate, and 2.5 percent reported that they had been sexually victimized by a staff member. In contrast, among inmates with a sexual orientation other than heterosexual, 11.2 percent reported that they had been sexually victimized by another inmate, and 6.6 percent reported that they had been sexually victimized by a staff member (Beck and Harrison, 2010).

An additional group of inmates that is widely presumed to be at increased risk of sexual victimization while incarcerated, but for whom there are not valid and reliable estimates, is transgender inmates. The advocacy groups Stop Prisoner Rape and the American Civil Liberty Union's National Prison Project collaborated on a 2005 report, which detailed the risks and susceptibility of transgender inmates to prison sexual victimization, but offered no empirical evidence to support their claims. Others have echoed these beliefs, but they also failed to offer specific evidence of the heightened risk faced by such inmates (Blight, 2000; Edney, 2004; Whittle and Stephens, 2001). However, research in California correctional institutions showed that transgender inmates are disproportionately victims of sexual assault (Jenness et al., 2007; Sexton, Jenness, and Sumner, 2010). In a set of interviews of thirty-nine transgender inmates and a random sample of 322 inmates housed in male prisons, 59 percent of transgender inmates reported that they had been sexually assaulted while incarcerated, compared to 4.4 percent of the random sample of inmates housed in male prisons (Jenness et al., 2007).

Scholars and inmates both recognize that a constellation of factors makes particular inmates more likely than others to be victimized. Wolff and colleagues (2007) asserted that targets of sexual victimization in women's prisons were young, white, and new to the correctional institution, with a history of sexual abuse before the age of eighteen years. Inmates in one jurisdiction were asked what characteristics they believed made an inmate a target for sexual assault, and the most commonly identified risk factors were "being homosexual," followed by "offense against a child," "offense of domestic abuse," "being weak or small," and "being a pretty boy" (Wolff et al., 2006). Interestingly, age and race, perhaps the two most commonly identified characteristics in research, were not identified by inmates as strongly related to sexual victimization. However, the fact that inmates recognize that factors exist that likely increase or decrease their likelihood of sexual victimization does not preclude recognition of the possibility of sexual assault existing for most if not all inmates.

Tewksbury (1989b) suggested that a significant level of fear of sexual assault could be found among inmates, with the highest level of fear reported by inmates who were physically shorter and heavier. Data reported by Human Rights Watch (2001) also supported the contention that fear of sexual violence was common among male inmates and significantly more common than actual incidents of rape. As summarized by Stop Prisoner Rape (2006),

> while anyone can become a victim of sexual assault while in detention, certain groups of inmates are especially vulnerable. Among the chief targets of sexual violence are: non-violent, first-time offenders who are inexperienced in the ways of prison life; youth held in juvenile and adult facilities; gay and transgendered detainees, or those who are perceived to be gay or gender variant; and, finally, those held in immigration detention centers. (pp. 1–2)

The research literature shows that demographic characteristics are especially determinant of an inmate's likelihood to be a victim of prison sexual violence. Specifically, inmates who are white and young are especially likely to be targeted. Further risk factors include being mentally ill, having committed sexual or nonviolent offenses, and self-identifing as gay, bisexual, or transgender.

Research on Perpetrator Characteristics

While the research literature has identified a consistent set of factors associated with increased likelihood of sexual victimization during incarceration, the body of literature is less well developed concerning characteristics of inmates and staff members who perpetrate sexual violence against inmates. As with the case of victims, perpetrators may be best identified (based on the existing body of research) through demographics. Age and race have been the two most consistently identified factors related to likelihood of perpetration of sexual violence in correctional institutions.

Whereas victimization likelihood is related to younger age and being white, perpetration likelihood is related to being older than victims and being black or Hispanic. Across all substantiated cases of sexual violence in US prisons throughout 2005, 51 percent of known inmate perpetrators were age thirty-five or older, compared to only 23.7 percent of victims being age thirty-five or older (Beck and Harrison, 2006). In jail cases, the numbers are slightly lower, but one-third (32.4 percent) of jail inmates known to have perpetrated sexual violence against other inmates are age thirty-five or older (Beck and Harrison, 2006). This pattern also holds for staff members involved in sexual misconduct and sexual harassment of inmates, as nearly 57 percent of perpetrators in substantiated cases were age thirty-five or older (Beck and Harrison, 2006). In Texas, Austin and colleagues (2006) reported that two-thirds (67.4 percent) of the sustained incidents involved perpetrators who were at least one year older than their victims. The mean age for sexual assault perpetrators in sustained cases was 33.1.

In regard to race, the national statistics regarding substantiated cases show that black inmates constituted more than one-third (38.8 percent) of known perpetrators. White inmates accounted for 43.0 percent, Hispanic inmates accounted for 14.7 percent, and inmates of other races 3.4 percent (Beck and Harrison, 2006). We must point out here that, whereas above it is noted that white inmates constitute the smallest group of sexual violence perpetrators, nationally these inmates are the most likely group to be substantiated as perpetrators as a result of investigation. However, this finding is not universal, as Austin and colleagues (2006) reported that two-thirds (67.5 percent) of the sustained incidents of sexual violence in Texas prisons involved black perpetrators. Data also show that not only are minority groups overrepresented among inmate-on-inmate sexual violence perpetrators, but so too is most prison sexual violence interracial. Most often black (81 percent) and Hispanic (67 percent) perpetrators sexually offend outside their racial/ethnic group, typically against white victims (74 percent and 60 percent, respectively), and white perpetrators most often (76 percent) offend within their own race. In summary, minorities are more likely to be perpetrators, as well as more likely to offend outside of their racial/ethnic group. Whites are less likely to be perpetrators, but when they are, they primarily offend within their racial/ethnic group.

In terms of criminal background and behavior while incarcerated, known perpetrators are more likely to have violent offense convictions than other types of conviction offenses, and inmates that have the highest rates of sexual assault also have the higher rates of other serious misconduct and criminal activity (Austin et al., 2006). Heil and colleagues (2009) examined inmates known to have perpetrated sexual offenses while incarcerated in Colorado, and they reported that of 142 known perpetrators of sexual abuse, 26 percent had also been convicted of sex offenses in the community. Finally, the use of weapons by prison sexual perpetrators suggests that weapons are less likely to be involved in sexual assaults in correctional facilities (32.5 percent versus 68.4 percent in the free community) (Lipscomb et al., 1992). Male inmates (48 percent) are more likely than female inmates (30 percent) to report that they had been threatened with harm or a weapon by a prison sexual perpetrator (Beck and Harrison, 2010).

As summarized in the review of allegations of sexual violence in the Texas Department of Criminal Justice, inmate perpetrators "are also older, more likely to have lived in urban areas, have been convicted of a violent crime, are in a higher custody level, and have served more time in prison than their victims" (Austin et al., 2006, p. 5). One issue coming to light in the PREA era, however, is that correctional staff members are often the perpetrators of sexual violence in prisons and jails. Even before the passage of PREA, between 1995 and 1998, the US General Accounting Office (1999) indicated that a total of 506 allegations of staff sexual abuse of female inmates were reported in just the Federal Bureau of Prisons, California, and Texas. Of these allegations, 18 percent (n = 92) were substantiated. More recently, between 2000 and 2004, the Bureau of Prisons reported that 12 percent of all investigations conducted by the US Department of Justice, Office of the Inspector General were allegations of staff sexual abuse of inmates (Office of the Inspector General, 2005). As shown in the Bureau of Justice Statistics, in reviews of administrative records (Beck and Harrison, 2005, 2006), across all correctional facilities, staff accounted for between 53 percent and 55 percent of all incidents of sexual violence.

Among correctional staff, correctional officers are the largest group of sexual misconduct and sexual harassment perpetrators (68.7 percent). Other employees account for 18 percent of incidents, and contractors, vendors, volunteers, and interns account for approximately 13 percent of all substantiated cases (Beck and Harrison, 2006). And not only male staff members are involved in sexual misconduct. Rather, and to some degree surprisingly, women staff members account for a majority of sexual misconduct perpetrators in prisons. In 2005, 62 percent of staff sexual misconduct incidents in prisons and 13 percent of staff sexual misconduct incidents in jails involved female perpetrators. Additional data show that, in the Federal Bureau of Prisons, females represent 49 percent of the staff members investigated for sexual abuse of inmates (Office of the Inspector General, 2005). Keeping in mind that a majority of staff members in prisons are male, females are significantly overrepresented among staff sexual abuse perpetrators. A majority of staff sexual abuse investigations involve cross-sex relationships; however, in the Federal Bureau of Prisons, 8 percent of all investigations involve male staff and male inmates, and 2 percent involve female staff and female inmates (Office of the Inspector General, 2005). The severity of prison staff sexual abuse of inmates is clear in the words of former Bureau of Prisons director Kathleen Hawk Sawyer. In 2001, she stated that "sexual abuse of inmates was the biggest problem she faced as Director" (Office of the Inspector General, 2005, p. 3).

In sum, perpetrator characteristics most commonly include being older than the victim and being black or Hispanic. Perpetrators of sexual violence in prison typically offend against inmates who are of a different race/ethnicity than they are. Perpetrators are also often incarcerated as the result of convictions for violent offenses, at least more than other types of offenses. Staff members who engage in sexual misconduct or sexual harassment are primarily correctional officers, and such perpetrators often include a significant proportion of females, especially in adult prisons.

Challenges with Reporting and Investigating Incidents

Researchers widely believe that one of the major practice and policy problems is that, just as in the free community, a majority of rapes and sexual assaults taking place inside correctional environments are never reported to authorities. A long history of free-community sexual violence research has documented that both men and women who are sexually victimized in the community do not report their victimizations to authorities (e.g., Du Mont, Miller, and Myhr, 2003; Rennison, 2002). If these individuals do report sexual victimization, they often only do so after a substantial period of time has passed. In the correctional setting, with even more to "lose," or at risk, if one reports, researchers suspect victims would be even less likely to report victimization. Even prison wardens believe that they come to know of only about one-third of all sexual violence incidents in their facilities (Hensley and Tewksbury, 2005a, 2005b).

According to prison and jail staff members interviewed in a series of focus groups by the Moss Group (National Institute of Corrections, 2006), a consistent belief exists among correctional employees that inmates typically do not know how to report an allegation of sexual abuse. Even if inmates know how to make a report, staff members commonly believe that many victims may be reluctant to report due to feelings of shame. In a similar vein, inmates who are sexually victimized during their incarceration often indicate that they do not want to be labeled a "snitch" (Listwan and Hanley, 2012). Inmates may feel that they are in some way responsible for the assault, lack confidence in staff confidentiality or investigative skills, or (especially in the case of female inmates) see sexual assaults as "normal" and typical in their lives (and therefore not something to report) (National Institute of Corrections, 2006). Further, according to Calhoun and Coleman (2002), female inmates in Hawaii reported that, if and when a female inmate made an allegation of sexual abuse by a staff member, they were typically subject to harassment and intimidation from staff members and that the women feared repercussions for both themselves and their families on the outside. Consequently, many instances of staff sexual misconduct behind bars were believed to go unreported.

When sexual victimizations are reported, they are often not reported in a timely manner. Austin and colleagues (2006) contended that, in Texas, a significant number of the allegations made by inmates were not reported in a timely manner, with only 30 percent of allegations reported within the same day, and many were described as absent of independent witnesses. Because of the delays in reporting, little, if any, evidence may be available upon which to base an investigation.

Additionally, some victims of sexual violence may be reluctant to report due to concerns about what will happen to them and what will (or will not) happen to their perpetrators. The available data suggest that while a majority of perpetrators in substantiated incidents do receive legal or disciplinary sanctions, significant numbers are not restricted, moved, or prosecuted. According to the Bureau of Justice Statistics (Beck and Harrison, 2006), correctional authorities reported that, among inmates substantiated as sexual violence victims, only 46.6 percent of prison inmates and 40.2 percent jail inmates were moved to administrative or protective segregation units. Segregation for perpetrators is more common although far from universal, with 84.5 percent of prison and 55.9 percent of jail inmate perpetrators placed in disciplinary segregation units. Further, in substantiated cases of perpetrated sexual violence, any form of legal action was initiated against only 31.3 percent of prison and 83.5 percent of jail inmates (Beck and Harrison, 2006).

A major problem with investigating reported incidents is that sexual assaults typically do not result in physical injuries. Only 15.4 percent of all instances of sexual violence reported to correctional authorities in 2005 involved any physical injuries to the victims (Beck and Harrison, 2005). Injuries were especially unlikely to be present for incidents reported in jails (4.3 percent) and for acts defined as abusive sexual contacts (3.4 percent). When injuries were reported, the most common form of injury was a bruise, black eye, sprain, cut, scratch, or swelling (Beck and Harrison, 2006). Across allegations of sexual assault in the Texas Department of Criminal Justice, Austin and colleagues (2006) reported that "injuries are noted in less than a quarter of all sustained allegations, and in only 10 percent of all alleged assaults" (p. 37). Similar results were reported by Lipscomb and colleagues (1992), which showed that sexual assaults of male inmates housed in correctional facilities were less likely than free-community sexual assaults to result in physical trauma to victims (75 percent versus 58 percent with no injuries).

These same difficulties also apply to cases of staff sexual abuse of inmates. Between 2000 and 2004, only 45 percent of staff sexual abuse cases of inmates investigated by the Bureau of Prisons were accepted for prosecution by federal prosecutors. The primary reasons that a majority of cases were not prosecuted were "insufficient evidence" (typically due to a lack of physical evidence) and the fact that, in the federal system, sexual abuse of an inmate is only a misdemeanor offense, unless force or overt threats were employed. (However, we must note that sexual abuse of inmates in federal contract facilities is not covered by federal law, leaving these cases to state and local prosecutors.) A review of cases across thirty-six correctional systems shows that, for 1998, the most common outcome of a substantiated case of staff sexual abuse of an inmate was for the staff member to be fired (n = 115) (National Institute of Corrections, 2000). The next most common case outcomes were staff member resignations (n = 49), staff member prosecutions (n = 36), and administrative disciplinary action (n = 9).

The research literature shows that the problem of prison sexual victimization is compounded by a lack of inmate reporting. Studies show that inmates generally do not report sexual violence because of a fear of repercussions and because of anticipated harassment, shame, or disciplinary action. Also, like many sex offenses outside prison walls, many incidents of sexual violence cannot be substantiated, due to a lack of witnesses or any physical injuries.

Future Prison Sexual Victimization Research

As discussed above, the number of studies focused on prison sexual victimization has increased over the last decade, seemingly triggered by the passage of PREA of 2003. Burgeoning research has examined the incidence and prevalence of sexual violence in correctional settings, characteristics of both victims and perpetrators involved, prison staff members' roles and perspectives on sexual victimization, the challenges of reporting, investigating, and prosecuting prison sexual violence, and the impact that prison sexual victimization may have on recidivism. Still, more scholarly attention and work is needed, in order to more fully understand, prevent, and appropriately respond to sexual victimization of inmates.

Intervention and prevention efforts are critical. Examinations of the efficacy of various prevention and intervention programs designed to address sexual violence in prison are not only desirable but necessary to ensure that the most effective and efficient strategies are adopted in correctional institutions. Such efforts are important not only for preventing, intervening, and responding to sexual victimization, but also for enhancing institutional administration on the whole. As argued by Heil and colleagues (2009), this research should center on the financial costs associated with sexual victimization in prison, compared to the costs associated with successful prevention and intervention curriculums. Among correctional administrators, sensible resource allocation may prove to be vital, in order to reduce and stop sexual violence pragmatically and to enhance overall institutional operations.

The further identification and refinement of a typology for both victims and perpetrators of prison sexual violence may also lead to improved correctional management, whereby inmates with distinguishing characteristics that increase the risk of victimization or perpetration are more closely monitored and differentially classified and receive services that facilitate their safekeeping. Once an enhanced, systematic classification of victims and perpetrators is established, the formulation of processes scientifically necessary to effectively reduce and prevent sexual violence risk can take place. Along these lines, as well as for other types of prison sexual victimization research, future studies will need to address the full range of inmates, including females, juveniles, and others with special needs (e.g., transgender and mentally ill populations).

More research concerning the comprehension and measurement of prison sexual violence is also needed. Specifically, the likely interplay between sexual victimization and feelings of safety, as well as the relationship between sexual victimization and subsequent victimization, subsequent perpetration of sexual violence, and subsequent offending following reentry, demand further investigation and refinement. According to Owen and colleagues (2008), future research may consider these elements in prison by redefining the unit of analysis in studies, such as surveying housing units rather than individual inmates.

The association between sexual violence and other forms of violence behind bars also necessitates further exploration. More longitudinal and qualitative research, as recognized by Wolff and colleagues (2007), is a prerequisite to better understanding the "causal and contextual processes" of prison sexual victimization (p. 553). With violence relatively common in many prisons and jails, understanding how one common antecedent to such behavior actually influences violence can provide important understandings and strategies for addressing such problems. In short, sexual violence in prisons and jails is not an isolated, unique event. Sexual violence, in terms of both its frequency and its consequences, is quite far reaching, and therefore important to understand and eliminate. Ultimately, increased knowledge that is focused on the phenomenon of sexual victimization in prison (and jail) will lead to safer and more secure correctional institutions that are enhanced in their efforts to turn out reformed individuals rather than victims and perpetrators of sexual violence.

4

Responding to Sexual Assault

Barbara Zaitzow

> Sex in prison generally means violence, power, manipulation, and denial. . . . It's a raw power game. If the predator senses weakness of any kind, any hint of confusion, ambiguity, liberality, or fear, he will attack. . . . Silence keeps these lambs penned, shorn, and butchered.
> —Steven Johnsrud, Stillwater, Minnesota (2010)

As an abstract term, prison is quite simple: it's a place where a person's freedom, movements, and access to basically everything is restricted, usually as punishment for committing a crime. But for anyone who has ever done hard time, a prison is so much more: it's a place where dignity, privacy, and control are given up to guards and prison administrators, where isolation and boredom can drive someone insane, and where the simplest of necessities seem like luxuries. Life in prison has changed drastically in the past twenty-five years. As a result of changes in legislative responses to the "war on drugs" and judicial decisionmaking, the United States outstrips every other nation in the world in the number of people it puts in its prisons. According to a study by the Pew Center (2008), one out of every 100 adults in the country is in prison or jail. Prisons are more crowded, availability of educational and vocational programs is being reduced because of financial crises, and inmate-on-inmate violence is increasing.

53

Prisons have real consequences for the people who enter them. When prison environments lack effective programming and treatment, allow for the persistence of dangerous and deprived conditions of confinement, and continue to use forceful and potentially damaging techniques of institutional controls, the people who reside in those environments face the harmful and destructive effects or consequences of such exposure. For short- and long-term prisoners, the incarceration experience takes a unique toll (McGuire, 2011; Murphy, 2012; Owen 1998; Willis and Zaitzow, 2010). In numerous locations throughout the United States, the plight of men and women in prison is going unheeded. Conditions of improper touching by persons of authority, sanctioned sexual harassment, unnecessary strip searches, and lack of proper medical attention or proper food exist in numerous prison locations. In addition, psychological coercion and threats of sexual assault by persons in authority as well as those confined in such settings create a constant, unending, and intense universal pressure on many incarcerated persons. Prison overcrowding has fueled one of corrections' ugliest realities: prison sexual violence.

Allegations of sexual abuse of prisoners are not unusual. Among the common aspects of incarceration for many women and men in jails and prisons throughout the United States are rape, coerced sex in exchange for favors, fondling, groping, insulting sexual comments, and voyeurism in showers, lavatories, and dressing areas along with intimidation to prevent reporting of sexual misconduct. Judging by the popular media, rape is accepted as part of the imprisonment experience, so much so that when the topic of prison arises, a joking reference to rape seems almost obligatory. Yet serious, sustained, and constructive attention to the subject remains rare. As Stephen Donaldson, the late president of the organization Stop Prisoner Rape, once said, "if ever there was a crime hidden by a curtain of silence, it is male rape" (as cited in Abraham, 2001). Donaldson was a pacifist protesting his government's bombing of Cambodia in 1968 when he was arrested on the White House lawn, tossed in jail, and, in his own words, "gang-raped about sixty times over two days," with the complicity of a Washington, DC, prison guard (Just Detention International, 2009). Donaldson was one of the earliest people to speak publicly about prison rape, founding the Prisoner Rape Education Project, which published practical information and advice on prisoner rape. He died of AIDS, the result of contracting HIV from one of the people who raped him.

What We Know About Prison Sexual Abuse

Prison rape is not a recent phenomenon. Fishman (1934), a federal investigator in the early twentieth century, documented a widespread culture of prison rape in which corrections officials ignored sexual abuses, predators went unpunished, and victims were discouraged from reporting the attacks to prison officials. Research has been conducted on a variety of topics related to prison sexual abuse (Dumond, 2003; Hensley, Koscheski, and Tewksbury, 2003; Struckman-Johnson and Struckman-Johnson, 2000; Wolff and Shi, 2009), but prison rape continues to be a taboo topic that is not openly discussed by inmates or staff. Although reliable estimates on the number of prisoners sexually victimized by other prisoners and correctional staff are not easy to find, no one who has any familiarity with US jails and prisons doubts that rape and sexual assault are facts of daily life. The shortage of information is, in part, the result of the challenges of collecting data in a climate of fear of retaliation and stigma.

The research that has recently been completed by the Department of Justice, however, provides the most dramatic—and officially accepted—evidence yet of a nationwide crisis of sexual victimization in US detention facilities. Here, the Bureau of Justice Statistics conducted a nationwide survey of inmates in federal and state prisons and in county jails between October 2008 and December 2009 and reported that at least 88,500 adults held in US prisons and jails were sexually abused during that time. According to the Bureau of Justice Statistics, 4.4 percent of prison inmates and 3.1 percent of jail inmates reported having experienced one or more incidents of sexual victimization by other inmates or staff at their current facility in the preceding twelve months (Bureau of Justice Statistics, 2012b). Female inmates in prison (4.7 percent) or jail (3.1 percent) were more than twice as likely as male inmates in prison (1.9 percent) or jail (1.3 percent) to report experiencing inmate-on-inmate sexual victimization. Most victims of staff sexual misconduct were males; most perpetrators were females. While some suffered a single assault, others were raped repeatedly: on average, victims were abused three to five times over the course of the year (Bureau of Justice Statistics, 2012b). The survey did not include minors held in these facilities, but in a similar Bureau of Justice Statistics report released in January 2010, more than 12 percent of youth in juvenile detention reported sexual abuse, or one in eight (Bureau of Justice Statistics, 2010). It bears repeating that this crime—a crime against incarcerated people who are in the care and custody of the local, state, and federal government—is underreported and that a cautious inference is that nearly one million have been sexually assaulted over the past twenty years (Just Detention International, 2009).

While anyone can become the victim of sexual violence, the most marginalized members of society at large also tend to be the most vulnerable behind bars. In particular, gay, lesbian, bisexual, and transgendered prisoners are disproportionately targeted in both men's and women's prisons (Man and Cronan, 2002). Consider the case of Scott Howard.

> Scott was a gay, non-violent, first-time inmate in a Colorado prison when he was targeted by members of the "2-11 crew," a white supremacist gang with over 1,000 members in prisons throughout the state. For two years he was forced into prostitution by the gang's leaders, repeatedly raped and made to perform oral sex.
>
> Even after he told prison staff that he was being raped and needed protection from the gang, Scott was told that nothing could be done unless he named his abusers—even though they had threatened to kill him if he did. Because Scott is openly gay, some officials blamed him for the attacks, saying that as a homosexual he should expect to be targeted by one gang or another. And by his account, even those officers who were not hostile didn't know how to respond to his reports, because appropriate procedures were not in place. They failed to take even the most basic measures to protect him. . . . Ultimately, despite his fear, Scott did identify some of the gang members who had raped him. Not only did the prison authorities again fail to respond, they later put Scott in a holding cell with one of his previous assailants on the day he was to be released from state custody. Again, he was beaten and forced to perform oral sex. Scott had a civil lawsuit settled in his favor recently, winning financial damages and seventeen policy changes that will now become mandatory in the Colorado prison system. Otherwise, however, nothing about his story is unusual. (Prendergast, 2011)

Not surprisingly, for both women and men, having a history of prior sexual abuse adds to the likelihood that inmates will be sexually abused in detention. The often punishing atmosphere of prison life resembles, in many ways, the abuse that women and men experienced in their own lives before being incarcerated. Part of being abused is learning helplessness—that they do not have the right to speak out about it—and that they deserve the abuse. Unfortunately, this past experience may be reinforced in what they experience every day (and night) in prison. While administrators rely on surveillance cameras, metal detectors, and locked gates and doors, as well as correctional officers to maintain security, prisons tend to be places where the strong prey on those perceived as weak and correctional officers as well as inmates quickly recognize such vulnerability in newly arrived prisoners (Owen et al., 2008; Santos, 2008).

The systemic problem of staff retaliation against inmates who report abuse was also confirmed in the Bureau of Justice Statistics study. Almost half (46.3 percent) of prisoners who reported to a corrections officer that they had been abused by a staff member were themselves written up for an infraction. Inmates reporting sexual abuse at the hands of other inmates were just as likely to be punished themselves (28.5 percent) as to get to speak with an investigator (28.3 percent). More than a third (37 percent) of prisoners who filed a complaint after being abused by another inmate said that facility staff did not respond at all (Bureau of Justice Statistics, 2012b). The fact that prisoners have reached out to corrections officials for help with their personal safety and their pleas have fallen on deaf ears and have been ignored is unacceptable by any civilized society's standards. The story told by Rodney Hulin Sr., father of a seventeen-year-old inmate who committed suicide after his repeated requests for protection from his attackers were ignored, is illustrative.

> My name is Rodney Hulin and I work at a retirement home here in Beaumont, Texas. I am here today because of my son [Rodney Hulin Jr.]. He would be here himself if he could. . . . But he can't because he died in [an adult prison]. . . . [At age seventeen], my son was raped and sodomized by an inmate. The doctor found two tears in his rectum and ordered an HIV test, since up to a third of the 2,200 inmates there were HIV positive. Fearing for his safety, he requested to be placed in protective custody, but his request was denied because, as the warden put it, "Rodney's abuses didn't meet the 'emergency grievance criteria.'" For the next several months, my son was repeatedly beaten by the older inmates, forced to perform oral sex, robbed, and beaten again. Each time, his requests for protection were denied by the warden. The abuses, meanwhile, continued. On the night of January 26, 1996—seventy-five days after my son entered Clemens—Rodney attempted suicide by hanging himself in his cell. He could no longer stand to live in continual terror. It was too much for him to handle. He laid in a coma for the next four months until he died. (Hulin, 2001)

Although any sexual contact between staff and inmates is regarded by the law as nonconsensual, former prisoners said in some incidents, the participants were unwilling, and in others, they were "willing." Most victims of staff sexual misconduct reported some type of coercion. Half said they had been offered favors or special privileges and a third said they had been talked into it. Nearly seven in eight in this category reported only perpetrators of the opposite sex (Bureau of Justice Statistics, 2012b). More than three-quarters of all reported staff sexual misconduct involved a male inmate with female staff. But perhaps more shocking is that even when authorities confirmed that corrections staff had sexually abused inmates in their care, only 42 percent of those officers had their cases referred to prosecution, only 23 percent were arrested, and only 3 percent charged, indicted, or convicted. Of those who had their cases referred for prosecution, nearly a third were actually allowed to keep their jobs. Based on the potential for retaliatory responses by prison officials as well as prisoners, one can easily understand why the vast majority of prisoner rape survivors choose to remain silent.

Those kinds of numbers have increasingly captured the attention of lawmakers, criminal justice policy analysts, and prison rights advocates. But government moves slowly; it's been ten years since Congress passed the Prison Rape Elimination Act (PREA), which called for developing strategies and standards for dealing with a crime that's rarely discussed or prosecuted. The act may well be a Band-Aid placed over a gaping wound. Certainly, it does not create the sweeping reforms that would address the underlying causes of prison rape, such as overcrowding, a malignant institutional culture, and apathetic facility leadership. And, without such reforms, the rape-prevention training programs mandated by the act will be unlikely to be effective. But PREA did accomplish two goals: public awareness and a message to prison officials inclined to ignore inmate violence.

The Correctional Staff Subculture: Gateway for Misconduct

Corrections officials are understandably defensive about the Bureau of Justice Statistics study that indicates a high incidence of prisoner sexual abuse in their facilities. To be "fair and balanced," I must point out that most of the men and women who work in US prisons are decent professionals who have never physically abused or intentionally degraded an inmate. But just as in Abu Ghraib, the absence of leadership, oversight, and external scrutiny can create a climate in which abuses will occur. As other human rights groups have noted, a contributing factor to the pervasiveness of sexual abuse behind bars is the tendency of officials to deny that the problem exists. In states that have been in the embarrassing spotlight (e.g., Alabama, California, Kansas, Michigan, and Ohio), this culture of silence and denial is conspicuous.

> A pervasive code of silence among corrections officials at the Corcoran State Prison in California contributed to the 1999 acquittal of four prison staff members charged with arranging the rapes of Eddie Dillard. A 23-year old, 120-pound, first time prisoner, Dillard was deliberately housed in solitary confinement with a sexual predator known as the "Booty Bandit," in an effort by prison officials to teach him a lesson after he kicked a female corrections officer. The "Booty Bandit" raped Dillard repeatedly over a two-day period, as corrections officers passed by the cell and laughed. The implicated prison officials were put on trial, but acquitted, even though another corrections official testified against those who were tried. Prisoner rights advocates blamed the acquittal in part on the prosecutor's failure to make the code of silence and culture of terror at the facility central issues in the case. It was charged that the corrections union, the California Correctional Peace Officers Association, thwarted the prosecution by instructing its members not to cooperate with the FBI and state investigations. (Parenti, 2003, p. 252)

Like the prisoners they supervise, correctional officers adapt to prison life in the context of both public and private worlds. Correctional officers work in an environment unfamiliar to the vast majority of US citizens. Even most people working in other parts of the criminal justice system have not seen this component firsthand. Correctional officers occupy a position of professional and public trust. They play a variety of roles and are given enormous responsibilities and the power to effectively discharge their responsibilities. These duties include security, discipline, treatment, supervision (of housing, work, etc.), transportation, and management. Correctional officers are in a paradoxical situation of being the lowest-level workers in the organization but having the greatest responsibility for managing and supervising inmates. The nature of their roles and attached responsibilities often places officers in ambiguous and conflicting situations with respect to inmates, administration, and sometimes themselves. Even the slightest tendency of correctional officers to exceed their authority, abuse powers, take personal advantage of their positions, or fail to discharge their duties should make everyone—inmates, correctional staff and administration, the public, and politicians— nervous. Cases of correctional officer misconduct can bring great upheaval within the corrections organization, a loss of morale among the staff, and a significant reduction in the respect the public has for the department. In light of these effects, should this trust be violated, the consequences should be severe.

Little question exists that incidents of correctional officer misconduct, corruption, and abuse of power—similar to law enforcement officer misconduct—have attracted national attention. Some of the incidents have been egregious, while the balance of the others range from serious violations of law to minor violations of department policy. Yet the attention resulting from such incidents is less significant and, oftentimes, diminished in its importance when presented to the public than the harm endured by the victims of such violations. Moreover, the "behind the wall" manner in which most episodes of misconduct occur and are handled makes public knowledge about such conduct virtually impossible. Grievances or investigatory procedures, where they do exist, are often ineffectual, and correctional employees continue to engage in abuse because they believe they will rarely be held accountable, administratively or criminally. If an officer is reported and punished, the punishment usually only consists of the officer being transferred to another facility.

Prison officials typically say they are caught in a delicate balancing act between responding to inmate complaints and protecting officers from unjust charges. But even when evidence appears strong, history suggests that department investigators give prison staff members, accused of wrongdoing, the benefit of the doubt. Corrections officials have closed investigations as unsubstantiated despite eyewitnesses, lie detector tests, video surveillance, DNA, or other evidence.

In a 2003 case, inmate Carolyn Moss kept an officer's semen after being forced to perform oral sex. The officer took early retirement shortly after Moss filed her complaint. Officials closed the case as unsubstantiated, department records show. In other dismissed cases, women had intimate information about the officer or contracted venereal diseases in prison. In February 2003, inmate Janise Leonard filed a complaint against an officer, claiming she had awakened to

find him exposing and touching himself in her cell and making advances on her. She reported that he was not circumcised. A logbook
showed that the guard, who admitted he was uncircumcised, was indeed away from his desk at the time of the alleged assault, according to Internal Affairs records. On Sept. 18, 2003, an Internal Affairs
report agreed with Leonard's claim of sexual misconduct by the
guard. However, a review committee still closed the matter as "not
sustained" without explanation. In July 1999, two months after the
state pledged to better investigate inmate complaints, inmate Char-
lene Harris reported she had been raped in her cell by guard Nolan
Ware. A videotape showed Ware entering her cell after midnight and
leaving a half-hour later. It also showed another guard passing the
cell and an inmate knocking on the door while Ware was in it. The
department closed Harris's sexual assault complaint as "not sustained." Officials did find that Ware violated prison rules and that
there was physical contact. The state police were not so lenient.
They arrested Ware on third-degree rape charges, a felony that carries a 15-year maximum prison sentence. He pleaded guilty to assault and battery and disorderly conduct in March 2001. He was
sentenced to two years' probation, and the department terminated
his employment. (Claxton, Hansen, and Sinclair, 2005)

In over two decades of monitoring prisons in the United States
and around the world, Human Rights Watch has learned that abusive
officers do not operate in a vacuum. More typically, a culture of bru-
tality has developed in which correctional officers know they can get
away with excessive, unnecessary, or even purely malicious violence.
In such prisons, senior officials have failed to communicate unequiv-
ocally—through training, staff supervision, investigations, and discipline—that abuse will not be tolerated. The failures of senior prison
officials in the United States are compounded by the absence of external scrutiny. Prisons are closed institutions from which the press,
human rights groups, and members of the public are typically excluded. Indeed, independent expert inspections yielding public findings are rare and usually occur only after the situation has become so
bad that inmates have filed a lawsuit.

Prison Subculture:
Unwritten Rules and Codes of Silence

Inmates in today's prisons do not serve their terms in isolation. Rather,
prisoners form a society with traditions, norms, and a leadership

structure. Some members of this society may choose to associate with only a few close friends (Jones and Schmid, 2000); others form cliques along racial or "professional" lines (Carroll, 1974). Still others may be the politicians of the convict society; they attempt to represent convict interests and distribute valued goods in return for support (Clemmer, 1958). Just as a social culture exists in the free world, a prisoner (and staff) subculture is established on the "inside." Membership in a group provides mutual protection from theft and physical assault, the basis of wheeling and dealing activities, and a source of cultural identity (Irwin, 1980). The inmate subculture helps inmates cope with the challenges, frustrations, deprivations, and pains of imprisonment that are part of the prison experience (Sykes, 1958). All these deprivations apply equally to female prisoners, and some may be more severe for women (e.g., separation from one's family; fewer leisure, work, and educational opportunities; and closer surveillance than men). For women and men, faced with years behind walls, life becomes a strategy for survival. To make it in this environment, inmates must adapt to its more unpleasant features (Zaitzow, 1999) including exposure to sexual abuse.

Prison culture is a factor in shaping the degree to which inmates (male or female) access justice and obtain assistance with a variety of issues and needs that arise during incarceration. Criminal conduct directed at prisoners by other prisoners or staff goes unreported for reasons that are unique to the prison setting.

First, inmates typically define themselves and are typically defined by others as being in opposition to correctional officers and even the justice system that sentenced them to prison (e.g., "us versus them"). An inmate may not report an assault perpetrated by another prisoner because doing so betrays a code of behavior that pits inmates against prison authorities. Consequences, such as stigmatization, harassment, or even violence, reinforce these notions. Consequently, although processes may be available that provide legal redress for inmates who are assaulted, they are not pursued because the prison subculture makes that pursuit unattractive or, at least, problematic.

Second, violence committed against inmates is conceived as unremarkable in the prison environment. An assault may not be reported by an inmate because physical violence is part of the experience of prison or because such incidents can be resolved by responding with further violence. This normalization and naturalization of violence enhances informal resolution of issues and undermines the formal systems that profess to deliver justice to inmates.

Third, common notions that "criminals" do not "deserve" justice—or worse, that sexual abuse is accepted as part of one's incarceration experience—may lead to prisoners' not challenging circumstances where they do not feel they have been treated justly because they perceive that they are thought of as unworthy of assistance. Such perceptions persist even though the "lived" experience of many inmates and the attitudes of those who help them are to the contrary.

Finally, prisoners have a tendency to "not rock the boat" and to not pursue justice by challenging unlawful conduct on the part of other prisoners and correctional staff, a tendency that is reinforced by prison culture. Here, inmates may be less inclined to challenge perceived injustices, as noncompliance may attract disciplinary action or result in help being withdrawn. This passivity is a barrier in postrelease life when the formally incarcerated person must be far more active in pursuing assistance.

The social worlds found in men's and women's prisons exhibit at least two key differences. First, the social climate of the average women's prison is, in comparison to even a medium security men's prison, far less tense; the institutions are far less violent (Gray, Mays, and Stohr, 1995). Most female prisoners come to prison because of a drug offense or property crime. Far fewer are violent personal offenders. Therefore, women's prisons have a less predatory inmate population than that found in men's prisons (Welch, 1996). Second, the functions served by the inmate subculture in prisons for men and women are different. For example, the inmate subculture in men's prisons exists largely to protect inmates from each other. The subculture also helps to neutralize the rejection associated with incarceration and provides a buffer between inmates and staff. In prisons for women, the subculture exists for these reasons plus an additional one. The subculture provides female inmates with emotional support (Pollock-Byrne, 1990; Welch, 1996). Gender differences may hold the key to our deeper understanding of how sexual abuse is defined, experienced, and responded to by male and female prisoners and, ultimately, by corrections officials and policymakers.

Sexual Abuse: It's All About Power

Inside or outside prison, sexual assault and coercion are about power, not sexual desire (Ross and Richards, 2002). People who abuse others

sexually do not do so because they are overwhelmed by sexual pas-
sion. They do it to dominate, humiliate, and inflict pain on another
human being in order to feel powerful or to gain status in a social environment that values violence. The term *rape* is most often used to
describe forced sexual contact, particularly anal, vaginal, or oral intercourse. But forcible rape is not the only form of sexual abuse
(Struckman-Johnson and Struckman-Johnson, 2006). Having sex in
order to avoid injury or gain protection while incarcerated is not the
same as having sex because the inmates want to; nor is sex in exchange for items like money, drugs, weapons, or other contraband
truly unforced. These are all examples of coercion or "survival sex"—
sex that a person agrees to because refusing could result in injury or
deprivation. Moreover, sexual slavery is also an ordinary occurrence.
Stories abound of prisoners who, once they are "turned out" (prison
jargon for the initial rape), become the rapists' subordinates, forced
to do menial jobs and sometimes "rented out" to other inmates to satisfy their sexual needs. No one, regardless of their gender or sexual
orientation, deserves to be raped or forced to choose between unwanted sex and harm.

Unlike rape survivors in the community, however, survivors behind bars often have no choice but to suffer in silence. Because of the
danger of being labeled a "snitch," fear of retaliation, and lack of
trust in corrections officials, most incarcerated survivors are too
afraid to report an assault and so avoid the limited counseling available from prison staff. This silence, in turn, leads to long-term emotional trauma and untreated medical conditions.

> On April 1, 2002, Penifer Salinas, a woman serving a two-year sen-
> tence for car theft at the Denver Women's Correctional Facility,
> was assaulted by a corrections officer. The sergeant in charge was
> aware that this officer had previously had sexual contact with at
> least one other inmate, and he was under investigation by police for
> stalking women in the community. The officer forced Salinas to
> perform oral sex and then raped her, telling her to keep quiet or
> "she would never get paroled." The attack left Salinas bleeding
> from her vagina. Fearful of retaliation, Salinas did not report the
> rape for months. When she did, she was provided no information
> about how the prison was going to respond. Instead, she was placed
> in solitary confinement, without access to her legal mail or letters
> from her mother, and was subjected to retaliation from other cor-
> rections officials. Salinas was not informed when the officer was

removed from the prison and arrested on the stalking charge. Now out of prison, she continues to suffer from anxiety attacks as a result of the rape and the manner in which she was treated after reporting it. (Prendergast, 2006)

Being forced to watch and participate in sexual violence perpetrated against other prisoners are also forms of sexual abuse and can result in psychological trauma. Witnessing sexual violence can be terrifying and leave the observers feeling powerless to protect themselves or people they care about. While some perpetrators of sexual violence enjoy the sense of power they get from humiliating and causing pain, individuals who are forced to choose between hurting another person or being hurt themselves may suffer emotionally from severe guilt and the loss of belief in their own human decency.

Survivors need multiple avenues to report a sexual assault, especially if they were raped by a staff member. Inmates cannot be expected to report abuse to an officer who works closely with the perpetrator (Owen et al., 2008). Because of the "code of silence," officers and inmates typically refuse to report on one another, leaving the sexually abused inmate without any options to seek help. For that reason, the standards absolutely must include an option for survivors to report to someone on the outside, so that facilities will be forced to take reports of sexual violence seriously.

Sexual Abuse Requires a Gendered Response

In men's prisons, power and respect are currency, and how one ranks may directly relate to assault and rape of other inmates. Although many different prisoner rape scenarios exist, a majority of male victims are assaulted by one or several fellow inmates, often with the complicity of corrections staff. While a generally accepted social stigma is attached to male homosexuality, in the particular culture of men's prisons, a peculiar exception is made: prison homosexuality is explained away as being a sort of punishment—a violent act against another inmate to permanently shame him. At other times, it is explained as an involuntary release: a last resort that the deprived inmate has no choice but to succumb to in the absence of a female partner. At any point during incarceration, but likely at the start, an inmate may be tested by another inmate (or a group of inmates), and his or her response will set the pattern for the remainder of the sentence. This "prison code" dictates that inmates must either respond violently to a confrontation ("fuck or fight") or greatly increase their chances of becoming regular victims of assault. For inmates serving even a moderately long sentence, violence becomes their only acceptable strategy to avoid predators. Even a person with zero inclination toward violence stands a good chance of becoming violent within this culture, and these patterns can continue after release.

> After the incident I asked to be put in PC and they refused, so I wrote the FBI, who came to see me but not before I was taken into a room with the "warden" and threatened [that] if I didn't tell the feds to forget the whole thing, my life would be made real uncomfortable there. So I blew it off . . . and I stabbed one of the black M.F.'s that raped me about six times with a pair of six-inch scissors. I wasn't caught and I don't know if he died or what. . . . I don't need the added pressures of being labeled punk. (M., Beaumont, Texas)

Prison policymakers can post memorandums that encourage weak inmates to seek assistance from staff. Yet those platitudes miss the dynamics of prison life for men. Prisoners who seek assistance from staff, in virtually any custody-level facility, risk retaliation from those in the prison community who adhere to the tacit convict code. Once a prisoner is saddled with the "snitch" label, other prisoners will ride him for the duration of his sentence; therefore, underreporting of sexual abuse prevails.

Both men and women prisoners—but especially women—face staff rape and sexual abuse. Correctional officers have been known to bribe, coerce, or violently force inmates into granting sexual favors, including oral sex or intercourse. And some prison staff have laughed at and ignored the pleas of male prisoners seeking protection from rape by other inmates. Still, in women's prisons, sexual abuse by male officers constitutes a threat for female inmates that the system has yet to resolve. Recently, the California prison system began rationing supplies such as toilet paper, tampons, soap, toothbrushes, and toothpaste in order to confront its budget crisis, a policy change that led some inmates to turn to prostitution with officers in order to gain access to these basics. Such desperation has been noted in women's prisons across the country (Gottesdiener, 2011).

Surviving a sexual assault and then navigating the health-care system to receive adequate counseling and reproductive medical attention is daunting enough for those who walk freely on the outside. For women in prison, these hurdles can seem insurmountable (Zaitzow, 2008). The risk of pregnancy as the result of a sexual assault is, of course, a concern for many survivors, incarcerated or not. But obtaining emergency contraception or an abortion, if one is desired, may be more difficult for women in prison. Because many inmates do not report the sexual assault immediately (if at all), using emergency contraception is usually not possible, if it is even available. Unlike access to emergency contraception, access to abortion by inmates has seen its way through the courts (Kasdan, 2010). Although the details can vary from jurisdiction to jurisdiction, prisons must provide access to an abortion if one is desired. Here, "providing access" can range from providing transportation to an off-site medical facility, to allowing for a furlough, to providing abortions on-site, although information has not been made available about the latter option to the public. Additional legal issues emerge for women inmates whose pregnancy results from sexual assault (e.g., who pays for the abortion, who provides counseling). Women prisoners should not be punished for the criminal actions of their keepers by being denied the ability to choose a safe and timely course of action if abortion is opted for.

In prison, the possibility of a coerced abortion can hang over an inmate who discovers she is pregnant as the result of a sexual assault by a guard. In a letter to Stop Prisoner Rape, one inmate wrote:

> A rumor had spread through the facility that I was pregnant. I'm not sure how the rumor got started, but medical staff came to my cell and forced me to provide a urine sample that they could use to test for pregnancy. They did not ask me any questions, offer me any support, or seem at all concerned for my well-being. That same night, three guards, two female and one male, came into my cell, sprayed me in the face with mace, handcuffed me behind my back, threw me down on the ground, and said, "We hear you are pregnant by one of ours and we're gonna make sure you abort." The two female guards began to kick me as the male guard stood watch. The beating lasted about a minute, but it felt like ten or more. Afterwards, the male officer uncuffed me and they left. (Hess, 2010)

As with sexual assault on the outside, many survivors in prison are too ashamed and embarrassed to come forward, fear that their claim will be hard to prove, or fear that their attackers will retaliate. In prison the fear of retaliation is heightened, as the prisoner continues to live with her attacker controlling her daily life. And inmates who report a sexual assault are frequently put in segregated isolation, ostensibly to protect them from retaliation, but being cut off from the rest of the population can be emotionally and physically draining, and terribly isolating.

> Any woman reporting that she had been sexually abused was given the same treatment. "If you dial the PREA number," one inmate told the panel, "it's a ticket to SEG [segregation]." Wendy Hobbs explained that in such cases segregation was intended to protect the woman from other prisoners while an investigation was conducted, and not to be a punishment, but that this distinction was lost on the inmates. The review panel discovered that when women in segregation were moved within Fluvanna (to the showers, for example), they were not only shackled hand and foot, but sometimes restrained with what the women called a "dog collar" and "dog leash." "The dog collar totally freaked me out," said one member of the panel. (Kaiser and Sannow, 2012)

For women prisoners who have experienced various forms of abuse during their lives either on the streets or inside prisons, the combination of fear, isolation, and the injuries incurred as a result of such abuse can be staggering.

For women and men prisoners, access to counseling after a sexual assault in prison is virtually nonexistent, is not confidential, and certainly is not a safe option for many survivors who must continue to live within the crime scene. Prison rape must be neither ignored nor taken lightly. The grave, physical consequences of HIV/AIDS and other communicable diseases, which prison rape spreads, follow victims and perpetrators alike when they eventually leave prison, thus threatening the health of our communities (Maruschak, 2010). The emotional and psychological consequences of rape harm ex-offenders' chances for successful reentry. Egregious or repeated incidences of sexual violence may even provoke suicide. Any efforts to create treatment and prevention programs that strive to eliminate the sexual abuse of prisoners will require a critical assessment of the dynamics of gender and the different impact of sexual abuse on male and female prisoners and staff members.

PREA: Is This the Answer to Sexual Abuse in Prison?

Sexual abuse of prisoners should be preventable. Efforts such as making sure the staff is well trained, educating the prisoners about their rights, eliminating de facto immunity for guards, and following up on reports of sexual abuse would go a long way toward prevention. Congress had similar goals in mind when it unanimously passed PREA in 2003. PREA aims to establish zero-tolerance standards toward sexual assaults, to increase data and information on the occurrence of prison sexual assault, and to develop and implement national standards for the detection, prevention, reduction, and punishment of prison sexual assault. The existence of PREA as a law, however, does not mean that the problem of sexual violence in our nation's jails and prisons has been (or will be) magically eliminated. In fact, the initial results of the Department of Justice studies confirm what inmates, prison researchers, and social justice advocates have been saying for years to no avail: sexual abuse in jails and prisons is a life-threatening reality that needs immediate attention.

Prison sexual abuse causes serious physical and psychological harm to victims; and the list is incredibly long. The trauma for inmates is no different than it is for those who are rape victims in free society: bleeding and bruising, insomnia, nausea, shock, withdrawal, anger, shame, guilt, humiliation, anxiety, depression, posttraumatic stress disorder, ongoing fear, nightmares, flashbacks, self-hatred, distrust, substance abuse, sexually transmitted diseases, suicide, and death. However, this trauma is compounded by the fact that inmates are powerless to avoid threatening situations and may often share a cell with the perpetrator or are subordinate to prison officials who may also sexually abuse them. "The opposite of compassion is not hatred, it's indifference," according to P.R., a Florida prisoner, who was raped by seven men at one time (as cited in Human Rights Watch, 2001). In a case involving a Texas inmate, Nathan Essary was forced to masturbate and perform oral sex on a prison officer. After reporting the abuse to the assistant warden, the same day he was forced to work with the officer who had assaulted him and, as a result, he was assaulted a second time. Essary filed a lawsuit against the officer and the warden and, in December 2004, settled the case, receiving substantial monetary damages (American Civil Liberties Union, 2004).

   In addition to individual harm, prison rape has a major effect on society. Victims of prison rape have higher rates of recidivism and reincarceration, a tendency toward increased violence, and higher rates of substance abuse. The costs of lawsuits, mental health services, and other medical-care costs are astronomical. HIV/AIDS and other sexually transmitted diseases like hepatitis B undermine the public health. Prison rape results in increased levels of homicide and prison insurrection. As most prison rapes are interracial, racial tensions are increased inside the prison, and, once the inmates are released, tensions are brought to the "outside." Victims of prison rape are often unable to reintegrate into society and maintain employment, which frequently leads to an increased reliance on welfare and an increased rate of homelessness. They have a decreased trust of authority. Additionally, prison rape undermines the effectiveness and efficiency of government funding (Dumond, 2006; PREA, 2003). Perhaps the most exacerbating element is that discussions typically revolve around saving money rather than helping people, as if 88,500 people being sexually assaulted in prisons and jails throughout the nation is a fair trade for easing state and federal costs. This situation is an embarrassment, particularly in a society and country that prides itself on protecting people's rights and freedom.
   PREA is better than nothing unless, of course, it represents the last gesture politicians intend to make in the direction of addressing the problem of sexual abuse in jails and prisons. And while PREA mandates state and federal officials to monitor, train, and discipline prison staff and enhance inmate security—all under a threat of withdrawal of federal funds or the firing of negligent officials—it cannot keep prisoners safe from harm. Despite promises (or threats) in the new law to take prison officials or state governments to task for failure to stop rape and assault, the real cause probably lies in a more mundane and intractable reality: inmates will attack inmates if enough of them live in sufficient proximity, with insufficient internal security, for long enough periods of time. With this reality always present, Congress may fund an endless number of studies, but we already know that the key variables are really the sheer rates of incarceration in the United States, the density of prison housing, the number and quality of staff, and the abandonment of any meaningful attempts at rehabilitation. If it is honest, the new Department of Justice commission created by the law will suggest what we already know is necessary:

that we lower incarceration rates, reduce the prisoner-to-space ratio, train large numbers of new correctional officers to protect prisoners, and abandon the purely retributive and incapacitative function of prisons. Much work needs to be done to ensure the protection and safety of all correctional clients in institutional or community settings.

Recommendations

To some extent, stopping prisoner rape is simply an issue of better prison management. In facilities where the chief official cares about the safety of the inmates and ensures that his or her subordinates take this issue seriously, rates of sexual abuse go down dramatically. This accomplishment comes about, for example, by providing vulnerable inmates with nonpunitive protective housing at their request and establishing confidential complaint systems that encourage inmates to report sexual violence without increasing their risk of future assault or retaliation, from any party.

Perhaps the most important thing detention facilities can do is employ classification systems that effectively separate likely rape victims from likely sexual predators. Segregating the two populations requires maintaining basic data about inmates; it also requires training staff to accurately assess incoming prisoners' various levels of threat and vulnerability. Prisoners placed in protective custody must be grouped by security level. A maximum security gang member and a sixteen-year-old first-time offender placed in an adult facility may both require extra protection; that does not mean they should be put in the same cell. Creative approaches to establishing paid work opportunities for those in "protected" units need to be implemented to ensure that additional layers of punishment are not put upon those who have done nothing to earn such living assignments and treatment. Recent innovations in facility design are helpful, particularly the use of pod-shaped configurations of cells rather than the traditional rows. But no matter what the architecture, effective surveillance of inmates is essential, and meaningful rehabilitative programs must be made available, such as general equivalency degree (GED) courses, which used to be much more common in US prisons than they are now and have been shown to reduce institutional violence and promote successful reintegration.

Some policies that could reduce prisoner rape need funding, and legislators are in a political position to help. Overcrowding makes the process of staff meeting their responsibilities more difficult, particularly the duty of supervision. But overcrowding is close to inevitable if we continue to lock people up at present rates. Offering treatment instead of incarceration to nonviolent drug offenders would by itself reduce prisoner rape enormously. And Congress should repeal or, at least, substantially amend the Prison Litigation Reform Act of 1996, which was originally passed to stem the tide against what were thought to be frivolous lawsuits by prisoners but which makes the process of inmates seeking redress for sexual abuse especially difficult. Finally, we need laws that increase the independent oversight of detention facilities, and therefore their accountability. The historical lack of transparency of US prisons and jails has been a major contributor to the widespread human rights abuses that the PREA standards seek to eliminate. Without external monitoring, officials who participate or acquiesce in sexual violence behind bars are placed in powerful positions and can act with impunity. Even the most outstanding officials often cannot identify problems within their own systems—shortcomings that an outsider often can recognize—and may not be aware of best practices from other jurisdictions (Deitch, 2009).

Policy Recommendations for Change

Although litigation, public education, and legislation have yielded concrete gains in addressing the sexual abuse of prisoners, much remains to be done. Ongoing and transparent assessments by prison and nonprison individuals are necessary to address the numerous challenges posed by inmate and officer misconduct. While not an exhaustive list of possibilities, the following is submitted for consideration:

1. Reduce the number of people in prison through
   • Reforming parole policies, including criteria constituting parole violations.
   • Releasing seriously ill prisoners.
   • Releasing people in prison on nonviolent drug offenses, which includes the vast majority of women.

2. Provide drug treatment and other services in the community to proactively invest in community-based resources to keep people out of prison and to provide for those returning from prison.

3. Assess the extent of misconduct by carrying out a gender assessment of the US correctional system and disaggregating all data (at the minimum) by sex, age, and ethnicity. The assessment should look at the following:
   - Applicable legislation.
   - Penal policies and procedures for both female and male inmates.
   - Programs and services available to women and men.
   - Access to health services.
   - Data on the level of gender-based violence in US prisons.
   - Parity between female and male prison personnel.
   - Codes of conduct in place to govern the behavior of prison staff.
   - Presence of complaint and oversight mechanisms to monitor compliance with policies, procedures, and codes of conduct.

4. Prevent and respond to gender-based violence by establishing
   - Codes of conduct with respect to sexual harassment, discrimination, and gender-based violence by prison staff.
   - Mechanisms for confidential reporting.
   - Legislation, protocols, and procedures for dealing with gender-based violence among prisoners, including preventive and punitive measures as well as protocols for care and referral of victims.
   - The presence of appropriate and skilled personnel to deal with gender-sensitive issues such as sexual abuse and other forms of gender-based violence.
   - A culture of zero tolerance regarding sexual harassment, abuse, and misconduct by prison personnel.
   - A culture of respect for the rights of prisoners regardless of their sex, sexual orientation, or ethnicity.

5. Establish national-level internal and external oversight mechanisms and bodies, including
   - Independent inspection systems and clear reporting and documentation.
   - Inspection teams with female and male inspectors, and inspectors with expertise on gender issues, in order to gain the confidence of all inmates to adequately address problems.

- Health specialists on the inspection team to assess prison facilities and procedures.
- Gender-responsive internal complaint mechanisms that ensure that (1) complaint procedures are accessible, are as confidential as possible, and protect prisoners from reprisals; (2) complaints are reviewed independently in order to protect female and male inmates from human rights abuses, as well as prison staff from false accusations; and (3) nonliterate prisoners are also fully able to understand and access complaint mechanisms.

6. Provide gender training to all prison personnel on topics such as
   - The basic human rights of prisoners and appropriate treatment of women and men in prison.
   - Prevention and appropriate responses to gender-based violence.
   - Health and hygiene for female prisoners including the provision of items such as sanitary napkins and adequate toilet facilities.
   - The specific needs of vulnerable groups of prisoners, such as pregnant women and mothers of young children who also live in the prison and gay/transgendered inmates.
   - The needs of female and male prisoners prerelease and on release, including secure housing, support for family reunification, and vocational training.

7. Increase the participation of government and community organizations by
   - Increasing the recruitment, retention, and advancement of "the best" prison personnel.
   - Providing services through these organizations to female and male inmates such as professional and confidential counseling.
   - Engaging government and community members in penal reform processes.
   - Growing public support for penal reform, by working with government, community, and media representatives.
   - Collaborating with these groups to raise awareness on gender concerns in the correctional system.
   - Promoting partnerships between the correctional system and community groups to monitor the prison system from a gender perspective.

The policy recommendations may appear overzealous and costly but prison sexual abuse takes a heavy financial toll on the correctional system through medical treatment, legal bills, and the high costs associated with isolating abused prisoners in solitary confinement (Kaiser and Stannow, 2010). Preventing prisoner rape will also help inmates successfully reenter their communities when they are released from prison (as almost all will be, eventually). Not only will recidivism be decreased and the enormous costs of reincarceration lowered, but putting more effort toward reducing sexual violence against inmates will lower the costs of disability payments, public housing, and other government-subsidized programs associated with the severe financial, emotional, and social consequences resulting from the lasting trauma of sexual abuse. The real horror of prison rape, of course, has nothing to do with money, and everything to do with the physical and emotional trauma that prisoners experience. It all points to a problem that seems to cost more to ignore than it would to treat.

Conclusion

Judges send hundreds of women and men to jail or prison on a daily basis, but the public knows very little about the conditions of confinement and whether inmates are being punished in ways that no judge or jury ever intended and will come out marked by the experience of rape, gang violence, abuse by officers, infectious disease, and never-ending solitary confinement. One of the largest obstacles to eliminating prison sexual assault is the "social invisibility" of prisons. The general public neither knows nor cares about the plight of the incarcerated and thus cannot demand that its government properly protect prisoners' bodily integrity and rights. Unless the experience of incarceration becomes real through the confinement of a loved one or through a family member who works day-to-day in a correctional facility, jails and prisons and the people inside them are far removed from the public's daily concerns.

We should never take for granted that preventing the sexual violation of inmates is impossible. Through a combination of tough laws, fair enforcement, thorough training, and new regulations that provide reasonable and commonsense approaches to cross-gender management and supervision duties in prisons, this goal can be accomplished.

But nothing will change unless politicians, departments of correction, and citizens are willing to recognize that sexual abuse harms everyone. The practice adds an extra layer of punishment to the sentences of those imprisoned in our jails and prisons, undermining the validity of our justice system. As a country that helped draft the United Nations' declaration of human rights (and that feels entitled to criticize the human rights violations of countless other nations), we cannot have our own exception for people convicted of criminal offenses. What happens inside jails and prisons does not stay inside jails and prisons. It comes home with prisoners after they are released and with corrections officers at the end of each day's shift.

To move past this, we must move beyond the simple numbers game of PREA and take a serious look at the values that inform our ideas about crime and rehabilitation. A start in terms of policy is simply to put less people in prison. Overcrowding is a serious contributor to the phenomenon of prison rape, and prison culture creates violent sociopaths out of nonviolent first-time offenders. Other alternatives exist to incarceration especially for those convicted of substance-abuse-related crimes. The next step is to examine our prisons closely and make the administrators who run them accountable, not just to the bottom line of operational costs, but to the quality of life of inmates. Our legal system needs to embrace its constitutional roots and uphold the Eighth Amendment rights of inmates; accepting rape as a part of everyday prison life is not acceptable. Most important to a new approach, based on restorative justice and rehabilitation, is that it must begin with an examination of basic cultural values in the United States, and we must make the leap to valuing a person's dignity and humanity even though they have been convicted of a crime.

5

Conjugal Visitation

Tammy L. Castle

The visitation policies for inmates in federal and state prisons vary within the United States. Inmate visits are generally supported and consistent visitation has been linked to a reduction in inmate misconduct while incarcerated (Cochran, 2012), as well as reduced and delayed recidivism postrelease (Bales and Mears, 2008). In most cases of visitation, physical contact between the inmate and visitor is restricted. However, some family visitation programs allow contact between the inmate and family members. Conjugal visitation is one feature of some programs that allows inmates private, unsupervised visitation with a legal spouse or domestic partner. Currently, five states offer conjugal visitation to inmates: California, Mississippi, New Mexico, New York, and Washington.

The history of conjugal visitation programs in the United States began in Mississippi. As Hopper (1969) wrote in *Sex in Prison: The Mississippi Experiment with Conjugal Visitation,* the correctional staff he surveyed reported conjugal visits being offered for African American males as early as 1918 at Mississippi State Penitentiary, also known as Parchman Farm. Parchman was built on a plantation and operated as a penal farm with racially segregated camps. Visitors were received in "red houses"—described as such due to the red paint used on the outside of the buildings—which had private rooms set up for the visitation (Hopper, 1962, 1969). The conjugal visits extended only to African American males "because of the common assumption that Negro men had an insatiable sex drive and therefore had a special need for the sexual outlet provided by conjugal visits" (Goetting, 1982, p. 54). Furthermore, racist notions that African American men possessed "superhuman strength" were common and conjugal visitation was thought to reduce violence in the prison (Hensley, 2002).

The informal practice of conjugal visitation continued only for African American males until the 1940s. In discussing its early development, Hopper (1969) explained that prostitutes were allowed to visit Parchman from the 1930s until the 1950s, when visits were restricted to spouses and female visitors for the purpose of sexual relations. As Hensley (2002) noted, the large number of families visiting influenced the nature of the program, and it came to be "dominated by legally married male inmates" (p. 145).

Conjugal visits became official policy in 1965 and were perceived as a method of behavioral control within the prison. As Hopper (1962) explained, correctional staff believed the visits were important for "reducing homosexuality, boosting inmate morale, and—in conjunction with the home leave and family visitation programs—comprising an important factor in preserving marriages" (p. 342). However, he noted that conversations with correctional staff indicated few inmates took advantage of the program in the early days, mainly due to the inadequacy of the facilities.

By 1972, the programs were expanded to allow conjugal visits for female inmates and new facilities were built with areas for children to play. The private conjugal visitation areas allowed married inmates to have sexual relations with their spouses, which was viewed by correctional staff as a logical extension of the family program and a crucial component of family preservation (Hopper, 1962). Although never a large number due to restrictions on qualification, more inmates began to utilize the program once the new structures were built allowing for more privacy between inmates and their spouses. Also, the extension of the family visits to three days encouraged more participation in the program (Hopper, 1969).

The Mississippi Department of Corrections continues to allow conjugal visitation today for inmates who can provide a legal certificate of marriage. Inmates who are in maximum security, have a documented STD or HIV, and have a rule violation in the last six months are not eligible to participate. Inmates are given one hour with their spouses and provided contraception.

Other States with Conjugal Visitation

A few states have offered conjugal visitation in the past that no longer do, including South Carolina and Minnesota. For example, Stillwater prison in Minnesota used to allow unsupervised visits with family members as long as they participated in counseling prior to the visit. South Carolina had an informal policy in certain prisons of allowing the visits to inmates (both male and female) who posed "a relatively small security risk" (Goetting, 1982, p. 56). Of the four remaining states that offer conjugal visitation, the restrictions vary and are outlined in further detail below.

California

According to Goetting (1982), the first conjugal visitation program in California began in 1968, under then-governor Ronald Reagan, at Tehachapi Correctional Institution. The program was called the Family Visiting Program, and old staff houses were used to accommodate family visits. The program was expanded to the rest of the state's prisons in 1971, with an emphasis on family preservation. For that reason, unmarried inmates also were allowed to visit with immediate family members. Inmates were allowed overnight visits in the apartments built on-site at each prison.

California allows both male and female inmates at all security levels to receive family visits, although some restrictions are in place. The California Department of Corrections and Rehabilitation excludes inmates sentenced to death, those serving life sentences, and those convicted of sex offenses. Furthermore, inmates with disciplinary restrictions are not eligible (California Department of Corrections and Rehabilitation, 2013).

In 2007, California became the first state to allow conjugal visitation for same-sex marriage partners and domestic partnerships after pressure from civil rights groups. As McKinley (2007) reported, threats of legal action from groups such as Equality California and the American Civil Liberties Union forced the state into compliance. The legal threats were based on the passage of an act in 2003 granting equal rights to registered domestic partners, and civil rights groups successfully argued that state correctional policy should match state law.

New Mexico

The New Mexico Department of Corrections established the Extended Family Visitation Program in 1983, also with the focus on family preservation and successful reentry. The program exists in four of the state prisons, and inmates in maximum security and those with a propensity toward violence are excluded from participation (Hensley, 2002). Inmates also must pay a fee for the visit, and although HIV-infected inmates are allowed to participate, they must receive counseling prior to the visit (Hensley, 2002).

New York

In 1976, New York became the third state (after Mississippi and California) to offer conjugal visitation as part of the Family Reunion Program, with the stated goal to "preserve, enhance, and strengthen relationships between inmates and their families" (Goetting, 1982, p. 58). According to the New York Department of Corrections and Community Supervision website, conjugal visitation is now offered at twenty of the state prisons. The facilities for the family visits include private mobile homes with playground equipment for the children, and the program allows visits with extended family members (Goetting, 1982).

Eligibility is limited to inmates who have been incarcerated for six months, while being in residence at the facility offering the program for longer than thirty days. In addition, an inmate must "exhibit a pattern of positive institutional adjustment" and "successfully participate in facility programs that address issues related to his or her instant offense and/or history at the first opportunity" (New York State Department of Corrections and Community Supervision, 2013). Restrictions include security level, assignment to a special unit, and disruptive behavior, while inmates with certain convictions (heinous crime or sexual offense) are given a special review.

In April 2011, three months before gay marriage was legalized in the state, New York became the second state in the United States to offer conjugal visitation to same-sex marriage partners or civil unions. Blain (2011) reported the regulation changes were initially made by then-governor David Paterson in 2008, although some time had elapsed before the policy was finally put into practice. In addition to participation in the Family Reunion Program, same-sex partners are now allowed to petition for a furlough to leave the facility in the event a spouse/partner is terminally ill.

Washington

In 1980, the Purdy Treatment Center for Women was the site of the first conjugal visitation program offered in Washington (Goetting, 1982). Similar to the family focus of conjugal visitation in other states, the Extended Family Visits program aims to support family ties by offering up to forty-eight hours of privacy with immediate family members. Inmates are charged $5 for each night of the extended family visit, and the eligibility requirements are more detailed than in other states. First, inmates serving less than five years can apply after six months, and inmates serving longer than five years can apply after twelve consecutive months of incarceration. If the visit is denied, however, inmates may file an appeal within thirty days of the denial. Restrictions include inmates serving a death sentence or in maximum/close security level, as well as inmates housed in segregated or pretrial confinement. In addition, inmates with disciplinary infractions or convictions for a serious violent offense may not be eligible at the superintendent's discretion. Finally, inmates with a history of mental illness or infectious disease (such as HIV/AIDS) must be screened during the application process (Washington State Department of Corrections, 2013).

Legal Issues

Goetting (1982) identified legal claims on conjugal visitation going back to 1958, when in *Payne v. District of Columbia,* the wife of a jail inmate sought privacy with her husband during visits. Since that time, legal decisions in most cases were argued on Eighth Amendment grounds as a violation of the prohibition against cruel and unusual punishment. In 1973, the *Virgin Islands v. Gereau* case affirmed conjugal visitation for "pretrial detainees held for long periods in maximum security" only (Goetting, 1982, p. 67).

The following year in Ohio, a federal district court decided in *Lyons v. Gilligan* that a lack of conjugal visitation did not constitute cruel and unusual punishment. In addition, the 1974 decision found that no breach in the inmates' and spouses' constitutional right to privacy had occurred by not providing the visits. No opposing decisions have been rendered since, and the state retains the power in deciding whether to allow conjugal visitation.

Criticisms of Conjugal Visitation

Critics of conjugal visitation argue the program is inherently unfair because in some states it provides benefits only to married inmates. Inmates who do not qualify to participate then may become frustrated or hostile from the perceived lack of fairness, which may in turn lead to behavioral disruption within the prison. However, several studies have found this not to be the case as the majority of inmates support the program regardless of whether they participate or not (Holt and Miller, 1972; Hopper, 1969; Kent, 1975).

Opponents of conjugal visitation programs also have emphasized health concerns, including the possibility of increased risk of violence to family members, increased risk of STDs—including HIV/AIDS—and the associated legal liability, and increased risk of pregnancy and its consequences. In 2003, the director of the Ohio Department of Rehabilitation and Correction, Reginald Wilkinson, argued that because conjugal visits allow unsupervised interaction between inmates and their wives, they "may actually lead to an increased risk to the physical safety of family members in some cases" even though no documented evidence supports such a statement (Wilkinson, 2003a, p. 19).

The concerns over the spread of HIV/AIDS are more legitimate given that inmates have higher rates of the disease than the general public, even though rates have steadily declined from "194 cases per 10,000 in 2001 to 146 per 10,000 at yearend 2010" (Maruschak, 2012, p. 1). Moreover, the number of AIDS-related deaths declined from "134 deaths per 10,000 with HIV/AIDS in 2001 to 38 per 10,000 in 2010" (Maruschak, 2012, p. 1). However, opponents of conjugal visitation argue that even though rates have declined, correctional administrators are forced to consider liability issues regarding the spread of the disease.

As Wilkinson (2003b) suggested, even though correctional staff may provide access to barrier methods to reduce the possibility of transmission, no guarantee can be made that inmates and spouses will take precautionary methods during the visit. McConnell (1999) outlined some of the legal concerns, including who is financially liable for treating persons infected "through agency-approved contact" (p. 128). In addition, a concern exists over whether the institution is legally responsible for any infection in larger society that directly results from the infection of the inmate's spouse. If so, the institution would have to consider paying for the medical costs associated with the disease in the infected inmates and spouses, as well as any infected children born as a result of the visit. Finally, administrators must consider the legal issues surrounding whether HIV/AIDS testing can be mandated for inmates who want to participate in the program and—if found to be positive—whether they can be excluded.

Wilkinson (2003b) also identified pregnancy as a concern with both male and female inmates. Again, correctional administrators are forced to consider whether they "have legal authority to exert control over the reproductive rights of inmates and their spouses" by enforcing the use of contraception (McConnell, 1999, p. 129). Financially the inmate lacks the ability to support the child while incarcerated, so the cost becomes the taxpayers' burden to bear, including the additional costs with providing medical care to pregnant female inmates. Lastly, given the institutional setting, moral and ethical concerns surround whether female inmates should be allowed to care for infants inside of prison.

Other concerns for correctional staff include an increased access to contraband, due to the unsupervised nature of conjugal visitation (Wilkinson, 2003a). In order to accommodate the visits, correctional administrators are forced to find adequate private space, which increases the "likelihood that items can be exchanged" (McConnell, 1999, p. 128). Thus, officers are forced to take precautionary measures and conduct searches before and after conjugal visitation to limit the introduction of drugs and other contraband items into the facility.

Finally, one of the strongest arguments against conjugal visitation concerns the "just deserts" model of imprisonment, which suggests that inmates are there to be punished, and these programs may "diminish the punitive effects of incarceration" (McConnell, 1999, p. 130). As Wilkinson (2003b) argued, a "get tough," rather than rehabilitative, paradigm is currently dominant in criminal justice. Accordingly, the public perceives conjugal visitation to be a privilege that inmates do not deserve, and one they would rather not pay for with taxes.

Benefits of Conjugal and Familial Visitation

On the other hand, some scholars argue the benefits to conjugal visitation programs outweigh the concerns. As envisioned by the correctional staff at the time of Hopper's (1962, 1969) studies, conjugal visitation was viewed as a logical extension of family visitation designed to preserve families. Hensley, Rutland, and Gray-Ray's (2000a) study found support for this notion as participation in the program seemed to promote family stability. As Goetting (1982) argued, many countries in Latin America have consistently offered family visitation programs for this reason. Although tough-on-crime measures are supported by the general public, as noted earlier, family visitation programs receive greater support. In Applegate's (2001) study on public perceptions of prison amenities, family visitation programs were strongly supported. Although evaluation research in this area is lacking, some evidence has been found to suggest that family visitation programs have an impact on adjustment during and after incarceration (Casey-Acevedo and Bakken, 2001, 2002; Schafer, 1991, 1994).

Some correctional administrators have proposed conjugal visitation as a method of social control in the prison, because it provides an incentive for inmates to behave (Balogh, 1964). Moreover, Burstein (1977) argued that because most prisoners return to society, conjugal visitation may provide a "normalizing effect" on the inmate, thus decreasing recidivism rates (p. 3). Some empirical evidence supports these notions as Wooldredge (1991, 1997) found that inmates who received visitors had fewer infractions while incarcerated. In regard to reentry into society, Howser, Grossman, and MacDonald (1984) found that inmates who participated in such programs had lower levels of recidivism than nonparticipants upon release.

Finally, proponents argue that conjugal visitation works to "reduce tension and hostility among inmates related to a long accumulation of frustrated sexual energy, which may lead to homosexual rape and other forms of prison violence" (Goetting, 1982, p. 63). In Hopper's (1969) study, the correctional staff held a common perception that violence and homosexual activity were linked, and the inmates who participated in conjugal visitation were less involved in homosexual behavior while incarcerated. Hensley, Rutland, and Gray-Ray (2000b) and Hensley (2000b) found the vast majority of inmates supported conjugal visitation due to the perceived reduction of tension in the facility. Furthermore, the researchers found men who participated in the program "were less likely to display violent behavior while incarcerate" (Hensley, 2002, p. 151).

The most recent research on the subject supports this hypothesis. D'Alessio, Flexon, and Stolzenberg (2012) addressed the debate by examining the effect of conjugal visitation on sexual violence in prison. The authors utilized longitudinal data on fifty states obtained from several sources, including the *Sexual Violence Reported by Correctional Authorities* compiled by Beck and Harrison over three years (2005, 2006, and 2007). Beck and Harrison (2005) distinguished between nonconsensual sexual acts and abusive sexual contact (intentional touching), with the former indicating contact between the penis, vagina, or anus—including penetration. Focusing on a three-year period (2004, 2005, and 2006), the researchers identified 5,330 total sexual offenses reported to correctional authorities, which included both categories. The independent variable was whether the state allowed conjugal visits, and a number of control variables were added: prison population, average daily cost per inmate, number of assaults, the inmate-officer ratio, the percent of officer turnover, inmates under the age of twenty-five, inmates housed in maximum security, and inmates who are black.

When comparing means, the sexual violence rate for states without conjugal visitation is much higher than the five states with conjugal visitation. The authors then analyzed two random effects models to examine the impact of conjugal visitation on sexual violence. In Model 1, the only significant predictor of sexual violence was prison population, and this variable explained 41 percent of the variance in sexual violence rates. In Model 2 when conjugal visitation was added, both conjugal visitation and prison population were significant with an increase to 49 percent in the ability of these two variables to explain the rate of sexual violence (Beck and Harrison, 2005).

The findings in this study lend support for Thornhill and Palmer's (2000) sexual gratification theory, which identifies sexual violence as "an alternative mating strategy employed by individuals when opportunities for consensual sex are lacking" (D'Alessio, Flexon, and

Stolzenberg, 2012, p. 3). The negative relationship between conjugal visits and sexual violence indicates that within the prison context the violence is sexually motivated, rather than power motivated as argued by feminist theories.

Conclusion

In each state, the responsibility for rules and regulations regarding visitation falls to the specific state's department of corrections. Although a number of states have allowed conjugal visitation at one time or another, currently only five states maintain the program. As the most recent research suggests, conjugal visitation significantly reduces sexual violence within the prison. Other benefits may include social control within the prison, lower recidivism rates upon release, and family preservation. However, correctional administrators must weigh these benefits against legal and health concerns, the smuggling of contraband and security required for the visits, and a public perception that get-tough policies should restrict inmate amenities. Given that the most recent research assessing the impact of conjugal visitation was released in 2012, it remains to be seen whether the findings will influence more state prisons to adopt conjugal visitation programs.

6

Gay, Lesbian, Bisexual, and Transgender Inmates

*Ashley G. Blackburn, Shannon L. Fowler,
and Janet L. Mullings*

The prison is a microcosm of larger society. Many of the same issues and patterns of behavior found outside of prison—to greater or lesser degrees—are also found in prison. Just as variations occur in the combinations and varieties of sexual partners in wider society (heterosexual, bisexual, homosexual, transgender), variations (albeit of a somewhat different nature) also occur of partner pairings among prisoners, despite the same-sex nature of the sexual encounters. By and large, the sexual culture in prison developed around homosexual behavior. This divergence from larger society raises questions about those having sex in prison and the homosexual nature of the institutional environment.

Early research interests in studying prison culture revolved around the sexual behavior of inmates. One of the earliest known works about prison culture, published in 1913, was a study of interracial sexual behavior among juvenile female inmates (Otis, 1913). Fishman (1934) dedicated a book-length treatment to sex in prison, while Clemmer (1958) dedicated a sizable portion of his 1940 study of prison culture to the sexual aspects of the prison social world. Since the 1950s, many researchers have delved into this topic (Fleisher and Krienert, 2009; Hensley, Tewksbury, and Wright, 2001; Owen, 1998; Propper, 1978; Wooden and Parker, 1982). What can be gleaned from the broad array of studies of prison culture is that the prison sexual culture functions in much the same way as mainstream sexual culture does, to govern and organize the sociosexual world based on rules, roles, and expectations. Just as there are heterosexual, homosexual, bisexual, and transgendered people in larger mainstream culture, these individuals fit into roles in prison, too. Prisoner roles serve to sort and classify inmates based on the activities in which they are involved in prison or on the activities they were involved in before they came to prison (Irwin and Cressey, 1962). Prison subculture redefines sexual roles and expectations from larger society such that a heterosexual male may be reclassified into a nonheterosexual role depending on his prison behavior, sexual and otherwise (Fleisher and Krienert, 2009; Giallombardo, 1966; Owen, 1998; Sykes, 1958). This redefinition of roles raises questions about what constitutes a homosexual inmate. Prison subcultural values may direct inmates to view one inmate participating in same-sex sex practices as heterosexual while simultaneously guiding inmates to view the partner as a homosexual. Inmates' preprison sexual identity (homosexual, bisexual, heterosexual) (Akers, Hayner, and Grununger, 1974; Propper, 1978) and conversations with others about sex and sexual behavior (Fleisher and Krienert, 2009) can have dramatic effects on the role that they ultimately adopt.

Prison scholars have relied upon two broad theoretical perspectives to inform us about the development of prison culture and inmate behavior: the deprivation perspective and the importation perspective. The deprivation perspective suggests that the behaviors, folkways, and mores that govern the prison subculture develop due to the restrictive environment of the inmate prison experience. After studying men inmates in New Jersey, Sykes (1958) wrote that the "pains of imprisonment"—the loss of liberty, goods and services, heterosexual relationships, autonomy, and security—forced inmates to adapt to prison life in a way that was relatively different from the free society. Many scholars have suggested that the lack of heterosexual relationships contributes to the same-sex behavior observed among inmates in same-sex institutions (see Clemmer, 1958; Fishman, 1934; Ward and Kassebaum, 1964). An alternate explanation of inmate behavior and prison subcultural development is the importation perspective. From this view inmates bring into prison many behaviors, attitudes, experiences, and group memberships that have an impact on their adaptation to the prison environment. Thus, inmates' sexual behaviors, practices, attitudes, and expectations prior to incarceration shape the prison sexual subculture and experiences (see Akers, Hayner, and Grununger, 1974; Propper, 1978).

While these perspectives compete for explanatory power, explanations that rely on the interaction of both yield the best results (Thomas, 1977). Men and women prisoners have adopted variants of sexual culture that are based on the culture they bring into prison with them. Like free-world culture, a common feature of the prison sexual culture for men and women is the gendered nature of the sex roles inmates adopt (see Fleisher and Krienert, 2009; Giallombardo, 1966; Owen, 1998; Sykes, 1958). Also, as in free society, a patriarchal nature appears such that male gendered roles receive greater benefits and preference in many regards (Fleisher and Krienert, 2009; Pollock, 2002; Sykes, 1958). Despite the fact that departments of corrections typically segregate inmates based on the presence of outward anatomical sex organs (Wilkinson, 2003a), these varying gendered roles develop. Each group—men and women—experiences prison in different ways, and the sexual culture has evolved differentially around these experiences (Giallombardo, 1966).

Sexuality in Male Prisons

Delineating Sexuality in Men's Prisons

An important issue in studying prison sexual culture is to disentangle the complex issue of identifying varieties of sexuality and characterizing what each identity means to inmates. In and outside of prison, assumptions about sexual identity, orientation, and behavior can dictate a rigid congruence between the three, with the belief that a categorization into any one of these determines the same categorization in the others. In reality, an individual's sexual behavior may not directly correspond to that person's sexual identity or orientation. Generally, a person's sexual identity is defined as the categorization into a specific sex group based on identification with beliefs, values, and behaviors of that group (Garland, Morgan, and Beer, 2005). Sexual orientation refers to the group to whom a person is attracted (Diamond, 2000). So the description of a person's sexuality can be based on identity, orientation, or behavior (or a combination of the three).

In the free community, results of studies using large national samples suggest that estimates of sexuality depend on whether measurements are based on behavior, attraction, or identity. Laumann and colleagues (1994) found that, among men, 9 percent engaged in same-sex behavior, 6 percent had same-sex sexual feelings, and 2.8 percent identified as "gay." These numbers suggest that despite the fact that many more men engage in same-sex sexual behavior, far fewer are willing to identify as nonheterosexual. Similar patterns are also found among male inmates in two studies. In Hensley, Tewksbury, and Wright (2001), inmates reported engaging in same-sex sexual behavior at a much higher rate (40.1 percent) than they reported having a homosexual (7 percent) or bisexual (23 percent) orientation. Similarly, in Wooden and Parker's (1982) study, inmates described engaging at significantly higher rates in same-sex sexual behavior (65 percent) than identified themselves as homosexual (10.5 percent) or bisexual (11 percent).

Within the male prison subculture this discrepancy can be explained, as many men involved in same-sex sex practices do not view themselves as homosexual (or even bisexual). Early research suggested that the men that participated in same-sex sexual behavior and still considered themselves heterosexual were called "wolves" (Clemmer, 1958; Sykes, 1958). These men were portrayed as highly aggressive in coercing or forcing other men to have sex with them. The men that the "wolves" sought out were often labeled as "punks" or "fags." Both of these two groups were considered feminine, in that the roles they occupied in prison culture functioned as "substitute women" for "wolves." "Punks" were considered men that were "turned out," or changed into nonheterosexuals inside prison. "Fags" were those men that entered prison as self-identified homosexuals or bisexuals and behaviorally performed in that manner.

More current research suggests that male prison sexual culture incorporates much more variation in sexual roles. For instance, some studies showed a distinction between aggressive heterosexual male inmates that have sex with other men and nonaggressive heterosexual male inmates that also have sex with other men (Hensley et al., 2003), while Fleisher and Krienert (2009) lumped all heterosexual men together without regard to aggressiveness. Additionally, the "fag" role has undergone modification from previous research. Prison scholars now typically distinguish those male inmates who consensually engage in same-sex behavior and take on feminine appearance. This category of inmates has been more recently labeled "fish" or "queens" (Fleisher and Krienert, 2009; Hensley et al., 2003) and closely resemble the roles that transgendered inmates might likely occupy in the current prison sexual culture.

Another refinement is that prison culture has found a role for homosexual men that do not embrace feminine appearances (Fleisher and Krienert, 2009). They are still considered feminine in a sociosexual manner but do not appear in such a way. One further addition to the sexually prescribed roles is for the inmate that outwardly appears heterosexual but covertly engages in sex with other inmates. These inmates are referred to as "closeted gays" or "on the down low" (Fleisher and Krienert, 2009; Hensley et al., 2003). While maintaining a heterosexual appearance in the short term is possible, inmates suggest that over time, remaining "on the down low" would become difficult, and such inmates' sexual orientation would become public.

Fluid Sexuality in Men's Prisons

Male inmates' sexuality can be fluid during the course of their prison term, changing from heterosexual to bisexual or homosexual identity or orientation (Eigenberg, 1992). A popular sentiment among male inmates is that the longer the time a man serves, the more likely he will engage in same-sex practices (Fleisher and Krienert, 2009). This suggests that the deprivation experience eventually takes a toll on inmates and increases their chances of participating in same-sex sexual activity on the inside. A common finding when asking men inmates to assess their sexual orientation when they first entered prison compared to their current sexual orientation is that a larger percent change their orientation as they serve their sentence. Hensley, Tewksbury, and Koscheski (2001) found inmates identified as bisexual and homosexual 9 percentage points higher later on during their sentence compared to at the start of their sentence. Garland, Morgan, and Beer (2005) found that 28 percent of their sampled inmates changed their sexual orientation.

Examining inmates' sexual identities, orientations, and behaviors, researchers appear to find that different factors related to the prison experience correspond to different changes in sexuality. For instance, same-sex orientation is associated with serving longer sentences and already serving a substantial amount of time in prison (Garland, Morgan, and Beer, 2005). Longer sentences are commonly associated with a more deprived prison environment, suggesting that this aspect of the prison experience can have an effect on sexual orientation. Additionally, Garland, Morgan, and Beer (2005) found a connection with security level and time served. Inmates that had been incarcerated longer in maximum security environments were much more likely to have a same-sex orientation as opposed to inmates in minimum security environments. Regarding sexual identity, the only significant factor to emerge was time served. The longer that an inmate served, the more likely he was to identify as homosexual. This supports previous research that "time will get you" when it comes to changes in sexuality among men inmates. Alternatively, in explaining men's participation in same-sex sexual behavior, Garland, Morgan, and Beer found that only the more restrictive maximum security environment played a role in explaining whether or not inmates had sex with one another.

Resisting Sexual Pressure and Roles

A major concern for inmates that enter prison with gay and bisexual identities is that they have increased odds of being targeted for sexual violence while in prison (Hensley, Tewksbury, and Castle, 2003; Nacci and Kane, 1984b; Wooden and Parker, 1982). The male prison environment is largely considered hypermasculine (Wooden and Parker, 1982). The prison subculture is constructed so that nonheterosexual, feminine sexual roles are developed in contrast to these masculine roles. Most inmates identify as heterosexual. So this larger heterosexual collective pressures some inmates into these feminine roles. Discussed above, these roles are the "queen" or "fish," nonfeminine homosexual, and the "punk." Likely targets to be pressured into these roles are nonheterosexual inmates and more effeminate, slender, typically white heterosexual inmates (Nacci and Kane, 1984b). Inmates entering prison as homosexual or bisexual are pressured to fulfill these top first two roles—"queen" or "fish"—despite the fact that they may not at all want to engage in sexual behavior while in prison.

When faced with this pressure, these inmates have several options. First, inmates can submit and accept one of the roles that they are being pressured to adopt. Many gay and bisexual inmates sexually accept the roles of prison sexual culture. Wooden and Parker (1982) found that of the 21.5 percent of men that identified as homosexual or bisexual, all of them were sexually active in prison. These men were not solely "passive" or feminine in their sexual roles. All but one homosexual inmate was anally penetrated while only one-third of the bisexual inmates were anally penetrated. On the other hand, a little over one-third of the homosexual inmates and all bisexual inmates had performed penetrating anal sex. Some homosexual inmates may find that accepting these roles can land them with greater degrees of status as opposed to being "turned out." For instance, transgendered inmates entering many male prisons learn that they can command more status in a "queen"/"fish" role as opposed to some other sociosexual role. "Queens . . . look, dress, and act like women" (Fleisher and Krienert, 2009, p. 68), likely violating institutional rules in order to do so. In comparison to the other homosexual/feminine roles in prison culture, and other heterosexual roles, "queens" sit above the others when it comes to status (Hensley, Tewksbury, and Castle, 2003).

As a second response to sexual pressure, inmates can rebel against other inmates' advances and seek a different sociosexual role. Once inmates begin to pressure other inmates into a role, no guarantee exists that the pressured inmates will be categorized into one of the feminine roles. A common alternative that correctional officers suggest to pressured inmates was to fight, with the appropriate caution that fighting was a rule violation that might lead to loss of privileges (Eigenberg, 2002). Many inmates agree that fighting and adopting aggressive postures are worthwhile efforts to resist unwanted labels (Fleisher and Krienert, 2009). Physicality is not always required to repel labeling into unwanted sociosexual roles. Inmates can also communicate to others they want no part of these labels by avoiding inmates known to be sexually active, refusing to discuss sex with others, and firmly expressing disinterest in any discussion related to sex (Fleisher and Krienert, 2009).

A third way in which inmates can respond to sexual pressure is by drawing upon inmate social support networks for protection. There are two options here—relying on older inmates' mentorship and affiliating with larger groups, social networks, or gangs (Fleisher and Krienert, 2009). Most inmates suggest that being taken "under the wing" of a veteran inmate allows for a mentoring relationship that is instructive in navigating prison culture. Simultaneously, younger inmates are likely protected from unwanted pressures from other prisoners. Inmates that affiliate with gangs may receive support as they would from a mentor, but may fail to present a strong masculine appearance. This may lead to a failure of support from the larger group in some circumstances.

To deal with unwanted pressure or sexual coercion, inmates can seek official institutional aid when available. If officials learn of a sexual victimization, or if an inmate complains about sexual coercion, officials may relocate his living quarters if the aggressor is living in the same area as the target. Inmates may also be transferred to new institutions.

If an inmate is sexually assaulted or is threatened with sexual assault, he can request segregation or protective custody, depending upon availability. Protective custody generally is considered single-inmate lockup for nearly an entire day (Fleisher and Krienert, 2009). In the past, large prisons commonly segregated groups of homosexual and bisexual inmates for protection (Fishman, 1934). Wooden and Parker (1982) conducted their research at a California prison where openly gay and bisexual inmates were transferred. The irony of being segregated in these communities of nonheterosexual inmates is that inmates may still be pressured for sex. Alarid (2000b) reported that in such a unit in an urban jail, heterosexual/bisexual men—normally associated with the masculine sexual role—were outnumbered by gay and bisexual/gay men who favored the feminine sexual roles. As such, inmates in these masculine sexual roles, in a special housing unit composed of homosexual and bisexual men seeking protection from sexual victimization, were pressured by inmates occupying feminine roles for sex.

Conclusion

Men coming into prison face a new sexual culture to which to acclimate. Their preprison sexual identity, orientation, and behaviors can have an impact on the sociosexual roles in which they ultimately settle. Additionally, the prison experience—custody level, sentence length, and time served—all influence the degree to which an inmate may switch his sexual identity and orientation or change his behavior. Over time, the recognition of greater amounts of variation of sociosexual roles has led to increased understanding of the ways men adapt to the prison sexual world by adopting a particular role and the pressures they may face to conform to one of these roles.

Sexuality in Female Prisons

Unsurprisingly, female inmates, and the prison culture to which they are subjected, are unique. Called the "forgotten" or "invisible" inmates (Zaitzow, 2003), women suffer differently from the prison experience and therefore their adaptations are often distinctive to women's prisons. As an example, the use of pseudofamilies is an adaptation to the loss of female inmates' "free-world" families. Not only is sexuality considered in these kinship relationships, but gender identity is also important. Such kinship networks are not as common within men's prisons, suggesting that these roles and behaviors result from a gendered experience of prison life.

Studies of female inmate sexuality have been conducted since the early twentieth century (Ford, 1929; Otis, 1913; Selling, 1931). While criticized for their methodological weaknesses, these early studies provided interesting insight into the attitudes toward sexual encounters between girls housed in juvenile institutions, particularly when these relationships existed between girls of different races. Since these early studies, numerous researchers have delved into the gendered prison experience (Diaz-Cotto, 2010; George, 2010; Giallombardo, 1966; Greer, 2000; Heffernan, 1972; Hensley, Tewksbury, and Koscheski, 2002; Koscheski and Hensley, 2001; Owen, 1998; Propper, 1978, 1981, 1982; Severance, 2005; Struckman-Johnson and Struckman-Johnson, 2002; Ward and Kassebaum, 1964; Zaitzow, 2003) focusing on how women's experiences are shaped by the physical, psychological, and sociological nature of their incarceration.

Gender Transformations

While social construction of gender is flexible both inside and outside of prison, such flexibility may be more pronounced in the unisex environment of prison. Within prison, women may experience both gender role and sexual identity transformations. The accompanying argot of female prison culture defines the existing roles in women's prisons and how women interact with one another through the roles they choose or the roles that are forced upon them (see Table 6.1).

96

Table 6.1 Gender, Familial, and Sexuality Argot in a Women's Prison

Argot Term	Meaning
Aunt, grandmother, mom, sister	Female roles in pseudofamilies
Baby, sweetie	Nicknames for sexual partners
Boo, booty call, boo fights	A sexual relationship that is not serious; altercations between these sexual partners
Box whores, canteen whores, commissary hustler	Inmates who engage in homosexual activity for material or economic gain
Bulldagging	Ploys inmates use to see their intimate partner (e.g., an inmate walking slowly on the "boulevard" to see their "baby")
Butch, daddy, drag butch, little boy, man, stud, stud broad	Male roles in homosexual relationships; inmates who are aggressive and masculine in appearance and behavior
Cherries	Prison virgins; inmates who have not engaged in homosexual behavior in prison
Dad, brother	Male roles in pseudofamilies
Daddy tank	A maximum security cellblock designated in the Sybil Brand Institute for Women (CA) in the 1960s to segregate and house "obvious homosexuals"
Dog, prison dog, road dog	A loyal, trustworthy, and dependable inmate friend
Dropped her belt	When a "butch" becomes a "femme"
Femme, girl, girlfriend, woman	Female roles in prison sexual relationships; inmates who are feminine in appearance and behavior
Gay for the stay, jailhouse turnouts, penitentiary lesbian, penitentiary turnouts, turnabouts	Women who have been "turned out" once in prison; these women are not lesbians outside of prison
Homosecting, playing, being together, I don't play	Engaging, or not engaging, in homosexual activity in prison
Kid	Young inmates in kinship networks
Pointers	Inmates who "look out" for other inmates while they engage in homosexual activity
Reckless eyeballing	Staring at another inmate for a long period of time
Runners, tricks, pen pals, sugar daddies	Men or women on the outside who provide emotional, but mostly economic, support for inmates based on a real or faked relationship; a trick is also a derogatory term for a female inmate who allows herself to be exploited by others
Square	Inmates who abide by prison rules and do not participate in homosexual behavior in prison

(continues)

Table 6.1 continued

Argot Term	Meaning
Trick book	Magazines in which inmates can place ads or answer ads placed by men and women outside prison
True lesbian, lesbian, gay on the street	Inmates who identified as lesbians before entering prison; these women may or may not engage in homosexual behavior in prison
Turned out	The process of pressuring or coercing an inmate into homosexual behavior in prison
Wife/wife; husband/wife	Core dyads; inmates who consider themselves to be married in prison

Sources: Diaz-Cotto, 2010; Gagnon and Simon, 1968; George, 2010; Giallombardo, 1966; Owen, 1998; Propper, 1978, 1981; Severance, 2004; Ward and Kassebaum, 1964.

These gender and social roles "are represented by a combination of appearance, behavior, and personality characteristics" (Ward and Kassebaum, 1964, p. 168) and can vary by time and place.

Owen (1998) and others have described the gender roles existing in female prisons, and they are not all feminine. In fact, a female will commonly take on a masculine role on the inside. Masculine roles, reflected in female prison culture and related argot, include the "daddy" (Giallombardo, 1966) and the "stud-broad," "butch," and "little boy" (Owen, 1998). At the extreme, women will not only act as a man would act, but also dress as a man would dress. Short haircuts, the wearing and "sagging" of pants, and the use of male boxer shorts and sports bras instead of feminine undergarments are not unusual (Diaz-Cotto, 2010; George, 2010; Owen, 1998; Zaitzow, 2003). These inmates will also copy masculine behaviors such as grabbing their crotches. In addition nicknames are frequently used by female inmates to further portray their masculine gender identities (Owen, 1998). While a female inmate's given name may be Alexandra, she may prefer to be called Alex in prison. As an example of how alike in appearance these female inmates are to men, Lindy, an inmate interviewed by Owen (1998), described entering prison for the first time and believing a boy was sitting at her table until a fellow inmate explained that the "boy" was, in fact, a girl. Lindy stated, "We actually passed words back and forth cause I just knew it wasn't a girl" (p. 78). Lindy's disbelief goes to show that female inmates can be quite convincing in their masculine roles.

Opposite to the more masculine identities are the "girls" or "femmes." These inmates continue the more feminine identity they had outside of prison. Their clothes may be more formfitting, and they may continue to wear makeup and jewelry, if allowed. George (2010) described how relationships develop between "cute little girls" and "boys, or prison studs," and an inmate interviewed by Owen (1998) described how "little boys" are desired by the "girls" because they appear as men. These connections create a semblance of outside prison heterosexual intimate relationships. Watterson (1996) revealed this quote from an inmate interview: "In our culture, if you ain't got a man, you ain't got nothing. And that model from the outside carries into this institution. People play roles, but a lot of it is just to fill out the public image the culture says women are supposed to project" (p. 297). This is not to say that two masculine inmates cannot pair in a romantic relationship although, even in this case, one inmate is usually more aggressive than the other and therefore dominant in the relationship.

Even confined women are not immune to cultural expectations of heterosexuality or, in the case of the prison social world, a masculine and feminine romantic partnership (Giallombardo, 1966). So what may seem like strict homosexuality from the outside is actually, due to gender transformations, more similar to the heterosexual relationships these women were engaged in prior to incarceration. Trixi, an inmate interviewed by Owen (1998), said, "I like my girls to look like boys. I have had femmes (for partners) but I like them to wear clothes like boys if they are going to be with me" (p. 144). In addition to these cultural expectations, a patriarchal framework can be found inside the walls of women's prisons such that "femmes" have been found to be more subservient to their "butch" counterparts. These concepts and others are explored in more depth in the following section.

Sexual Identities

Not only are gender roles fluid in the prison environment, but female inmates can experiment with their sexual identities as well. In their study on inmate homosexual behavior, Koscheski and Hensley

(2001) surveyed 245 female inmates as to their sexual orientation before coming to prison and their sexual orientation while in prison. Before being imprisoned, 64 percent of the inmates reported being heterosexual, 28 percent reported being bisexual, and 8 percent reported being lesbians. Interestingly, inmate responses shifted when asked about sexual orientation while incarcerated. In prison, 55 percent reported being heterosexual, 31 percent reported being bisexual, and 13 percent reported being lesbians. These findings support the notion that sexual identities are indeed flexible within the prison environment, although this fluidity is not likely to occur elsewhere.

Past research has found that a significant predictor of homosexual behavior in prison is whether the inmate participated in homosexual behavior outside of prison (Propper, 1978). However, not all inmates participate in homosexual behavior while in prison even if they identify as lesbians and even if that self-identification preceded their incarceration. Women prisoners who identify as "straight" outside of prison often find themselves lonely and curious about intimate relationships and may therefore participate in romantic relationships as situational homosexuals (Severance, 2005). Such activity has been suggested to result from the deprivation of heterosexual romantic relationships (Ward and Kassebaum, 1964). These inmates are often referred to as being "gay for the stay," a somewhat derogatory phrase indicating that once the inmate, or "penitentiary lesbian," is released, any sexual and related emotional ties built with other inmates will be strictly left behind. Prison can be a confusing time for some inmates as they begin to question their sexual identity and what that means for them, not only on the inside, but also on the outside upon release (Diaz-Cotto, 2010; Severance, 2005).

While sexual relationships between inmates are strictly against prison policy, past research has found that consensual sex is quite common among female prisoners (Diaz-Cotto, 2010; Giallombardo, 1966; George, 2010; Koscheski and Hensley, 2001; Owen, 1998; Pardue, Arrigo, and Murphy, 2011; Propper, 1978; Severance, 2005). While consensual, the "butch" inmates tend to benefit more from these relationships. They not only have the ability to have multiple partners, but are also entitled to their "femme" partners' material possessions and items purchased from the commissary (Pollock, 2002). This perk is a prime example of how patriarchal beliefs have infiltrated prisons for women.

Past research reveals that, like men, women fear being sexually assaulted or approached by "butch" inmates for a sexual relationship. Owen (1998) quoted an inmate named Bonnie as she described her fear while handcuffed to a lesbian on the prison bus. Inmates have also reported being told that they will have to give in to sexual pressure or fight (Diaz-Cotto, 2010; George, 2010; Owen, 1998). Their experiences seem very similar to what men have experienced in prison. Although the fear is not without cause, George (2010) and Diaz-Cotto (2010) suggest that, as long as women make it clear that they are not interested, or that they "don't play," they will generally be left alone.

Models or variations of adaptation among women prisoners were first developed in the 1930s (see R. S. Jones, 1993; Selling, 1931). More recently, Pardue, Arrigo, and Murphy (2011) developed a more comprehensive typology of sexual behavior in women's prisons. Their classification system consists of five types of behavior on a continuum from no sexual behavior to violent sexual behavior: (1) suppressed sexuality, (2) autoeroticism, (3) consensual "true" homosexuality, (4) consensual "situational" homosexuality, and (5) sexual violence. Suppressed sexuality refers to inmates who do not engage in any sexual acts while in prison. These inmates are more likely to participate in asexual familial relationships. These surrogate families, or kinship networks, will be discussed in more detail later. The autoerotic inmate is sexually intimate only with herself through masturbation or other means. In a study on autoeroticism in a female prison, Hensley, Tewksbury, and Koscheski (2001) found that 66 percent of the female inmate respondents reported masturbating while in prison. Of these women, 18.6 percent masturbated multiple times a week. Writing about her experiences in a female prison, George (2010) also referenced masturbation. She described how long-term inmates, or "lifers," prefer to have a relationship with their showerhead, or "straight shooter," as it provides sexual satisfaction and relaxation without having to contend with the relationship drama. As most fights that occur within women's prisons are said to stem from jealousy or other relationship issues, some women just prefer to not become involved intimately with other inmates (George, 2010; Owen, 1998; Pollock, 1998).

Pardue, Arrigo, and Murphy's (2011) third category is the consensual "true" homosexual. These relationships refer to "true lesbians" engaging in consensual sexual activity and forming core dyads (e.g., wife/wife, husband/wife). The fourth category also involves consensual sexual activity, but this activity is between inmates who are "gay for the stay," or only participating in homosexual behavior because they are in prison. The last category recognizes that sexual violence does occur among female inmates as well as between female inmates and staff members. According to Pardue, Arrigo, and Murphy, sexual violence in a women's prison can occur through manipulation, compliance, and psychological and physical coercion. For example, inmates referred to as "toughies" are known to exploit weak inmates to benefit themselves sexually, financially, or otherwise.

While most prisons do not segregate lesbian inmates unless an articulated risk or history of predatory behavior is present, examples exist of female prisons using segregation to control homosexuality and the threat of sexual assault. Diaz-Cotto (2010) describes the "Daddy Tank," or Cell Block 4200, as it existed in California's Sybil Brand Institute for Women beginning in the 1960s. Segregation in the "Daddy Tank" was based on a California state law that "required the separation or 'exclusion' of identified lesbians from other prisoners" (Diaz-Cotto, 2010, p. 139), a practice that did not formally end until 1986. Not only were segregated inmates severely restricted, but they were also reportedly mistreated by correctional staff. In 1976, lesbian inmates were moved to a dormitory setting that included both "butch" and "femme" inmates; however, housing these inmates together only served to increase sexual activity. While this type of segregation is not common, another popular method of control is managing placement of inmates. When two inmates are found to be in a relationship, prison authorities may break up the dyad, moving one of the inmates to another part of the prison.

Female inmates not only use their sexuality in a coercive way within the prison, but are also known to manipulate vulnerable individuals in the community as a means to financial gain. While not all relationships established between female inmates and individuals on the outside are coercive, or based on falsities, in a well-known practice, some women respond to advertisements or seek a "pen pal" in order to lead a man, or woman, on. The inmate may fake emotional interest and even promise to continue the relationship once released, while, in reality, they have no intention of doing so. These outsiders are known as "tricks" or "sugar daddies" among the inmates, and some inmates may have multiple "tricks" at one time (Owen, 1998). Women prisoners are motivated to engage in this behavior due to the financial support that comes along with establishing and maintaining the relationship.

Constructs of gender and sexuality in women's prisons can be complicated by and are certainly situated within the prison experience. A woman may enter prison with one identity but, over time, find that another identity may help her to better adapt or cope with the prison environment. While these identities can lead to sexual relationships with fellow inmates and others, relationships between inmates that are not sexual at all are not uncommon. Like sexual relationships, however, these too suggest the fluidity of gender identities among female inmates.

Pseudofamilies

Surrogate families, kinship networks, or pseudofamilies, as they are most well known as, are a socially constructed phenomenon that has been studied and written about since the earliest studies on the social nature of women's prisons (Giallombardo, 1966; Heffernan, 1972; R. S. Jones, 1993; Owen, 1998; Propper, 1982; Selling, 1931). As homosexual relationships develop due to the deprivation of heterosexual relationships in prison, pseudofamilies have been explained as an adaptation to the lack of outside familial relationships. Many female inmates lose even their strongest connections to family the longer they are incarcerated. Whether the reason is location, cost, or emotional difficulty, sustaining close relationships with loved ones once in prison can be challenging (Owen, 1998). Due to losing these close connections, female inmates begin to create their own prison families with fellow inmates. These relationships provide female inmates with the emotional support they need to cope with the prison environment as well as assistance with routine responsibilities (Heffernan, 1972; Propper, 1982). While originally these relationships were thought to be sexual in nature, in the 1970s and 1980s this assumption came into question, leading to an understanding of surrogate families that reaches beyond sexuality (Bosworth, 1999; Hensley, 2002; R. S. Jones, 1993; Propper, 1982). Instead, these relationships have been found to be developed based on friendship, love, respect, and loyalty for one another.

As one might expect, pseudofamilies among female inmates are matrilineal in structure with an older, long-term inmate taking the lead role of "mom." Beyond the role of "mom," most other familial roles are represented as well. As Gagnon and Simon (1968) and others have discussed, other roles include "fathers," "daughters," "brothers," "sisters," "aunts," "cousins," and "grandmothers." Relating these to the prison roles discussed above, "stud-broads" or "butch" inmates take on the male roles in the family, as "father," "brother," or "son." "Femmes" are "sisters" and "aunts." Whereas "moms" and "grandmothers" are wise to the prison social world, younger inmates who are less experienced with the prison environment are known as "kids" and supervised and mentored as such. Partnerships are also evident inside and outside of the pseudofamily structure. For example, a husband/wife or wife/wife core dyad may form the foundation of the family. These dyads may be sexual but, as was discussed above, a physical relationship is not necessary (Diaz-Cotto, 2010). In addition, one woman alone could form and be the head of the family. Partnerships outside of the pseudofamily are in the form of friendships. Women who are close friends may call each other their "dog" (Owen, 1998). Variations of this are "road dog" and "prison dog." "Dog" is by no means a derogatory term in these cases. Generally these women have served many years together, perhaps one has mentored the other, and over time they have developed a close friendship in which there is trust and loyalty.

While in the mid-twentieth century pseudofamilies were found to be quite prevalent and secure in their various structures, more recent research has revealed that pseudofamily existence may be less customary. In her interviews with women inmates in California, Owen (1998) found that a "significant minority" of inmates did not participate in familial or emotionally laden relationships with other prisoners. This disconnect is especially true if the woman is serving a short sentence and does not identify with a criminal lifestyle or the prison culture. When such relationships were found, they were usually among inmates new to the prison and were not reported to last long. Greer (2000) reported similar findings; inmates in her study suggested "doing your own time," or not getting involved with other inmates, as the way to avoid trouble.

One reason for the decline in pseudofamilies among female inmates is the change in cultural expectations for women in general during the latter half of the twentieth century. This shift led to less connection with and reliance upon traditional social roles. Greer

(2000) found that women prisoners today tend to be more individually focused rather than having an identity that is formed through social expectations and resulting relationships. A second reason is that today's female prison culture is more similar to male prison culture with its lack of trust and emotional bonding (Greer, 2000). As more women enter prisons for longer sentences, women's prisons have grown from the small cottage-style arrangements to prison facilities that mirror male facilities in build and security measures (e.g., razor wire, cell blocks, administrative segregation). The female offender has also changed. No longer is she docile. Instead, women entering prison today are more likely than they were in the past to be aggressive, exploitative, and troublesome for prison authorities.

At one point in time, pseudofamilies were said to be the "primary social unit" within the female prison culture, reflecting the domestic roles that were most important to women on the outside (Owen, 1998). Due to the changing nature of the cultural landscape both inside and outside of the prison, some women seem to be less inclined to take part in familial-style relationships or make any deep emotional connections while they serve their time. While pseudofamilies and other relationships built on deep emotional connections may never disappear completely from the female prison culture, in today's female prisons, the need for and desire to establish such connections seem to be waning.

Conclusion

The study of gender and sexual identities is complicated, especially for female inmates. Not only are gender and sexual identity transformations common among women prisoners, but the resulting behavior and building of relationships contribute significantly to the female prison culture. Subcultural roles and argot suggest that such transformations are to be expected as they are the most utilized way to normalize the prison environment to reflect the lives led by female inmates prior to being incarcerated.

Challenges Posed and Faced by the Transgender Inmate

The management of transgender prison inmates poses a challenge for prison officials (Petersen et al., 1996). Recent court rulings and related settlements not only have brought transgender inmates to the forefront, but point to specific areas from which the more significant management difficulties arise. We must note that little consensus can be found on the definition of and use of the term *transgender* (Sexton, Jenness, and Sumner, 2010). While some delineate between transgender and transsexual, with transsexuals having taken the step to use hormone treatments and surgical procedures to change their outward appearance, many times these terms are used interchangeably. A person who is born female but changes his outward appearance to become male is referred to as a "transman" while a person who is born male and changes to a female identity is referred to as a "transwoman" (Leach, 2007). Regarding sexuality and sexual orientation, transgendered inmates, like other inmates, may be straight, gay, lesbian, or bisexual. This further element adds another layer of difficulty when prison officials attempt to make management decisions regarding this population.

Sexual Victimization

Transgendered inmates, transwomen in particular, are more likely to be sexually abused and assaulted once incarcerated (Jenness et al., 2010). This increased risk may be due to their physical appearance and demeanor at the time they enter prison. In the single-sex environment of the male prison, a feminine inmate may draw unwanted attention. In this sense, transwomen are vulnerable to unwanted sex in a population of male inmates looking for what they perceive to be a heterosexual-like encounter. While transwomen are certainly found with the general population of male prisons, due to their risk of being sexually assaulted, transwomen inmates may be segregated for their own protection. When they are not provided this layer of protection, the door is opened for legal repercussions.

The most well-known Supreme Court case involving a transgender inmate is that of *Farmer v. Brennan* (1994). Farmer, a transwoman, suffered numerous violent sexual attacks when housed in the general population, eventually acquiring HIV. While the Court did not side with Farmer, in their decision they established the standard of "deliberate indifference" to inmate risk. If correctional authorities know that an inmate is at risk for victimization and are deliberately indifferent to the situation, they may be held liable if the inmate is in fact victimized while under their supervision. A similar case is that of

Alexis Giraldo, also a transwoman, who was sexually victimized while incarcerated in California. In this case, the result was a settlement of $10,000 ("California Pays," 2012).

Medical Treatment

While risk of victimization, particularly among transgender inmates, is one area of concern, another is that of medical treatment for gender identity disorder. Such treatment is specific to transgender prisoners. Gender identity disorder is a diagnosis recognized by the American Psychological Association and defined within the *Diagnostic and Statistical Manual of Mental Disorders,* fourth edition (DSM-IV). Questions of treatment are generally based on this diagnosis. While transgender individuals may already dress and behave in the gender role with which they identify, nonsurgical and surgical therapeutic options also exist for the treatment of gender identity disorder. While counseling is essential to the treatment process, a popular option that induces actual physical change to the body is hormone therapy. In fact, such therapy is where the sex change process begins. Some transgender individuals may feel that hormone therapy is not enough and, when the option is available to them, may consider gender reassignment surgery. For a transwoman, the penis can be the ultimate reminder that they were born in the wrong body. This crisis in identity has led to attempts at self-castration and other acts of self-harm when surgical options are inaccessible, as was the case with Michelle Kosilek.

In 2012, a federal court ruled that Michelle Kosilek, a prisoner in Massachusetts serving a life sentence for the murder of her wife, can receive sex reassignment surgery while imprisoned (Lavoie, 2012). The ruling was based on the requirement that institutions provide effective treatment for a serious medical condition. The medical condition in this case was gender identity disorder leading to numerous attempts at self-harm. A related case is that of Donna Dawn Konitzer, a prisoner in Wisconsin. Konitzer's case is well known due to Wisconsin's passing the Sex Change Prevention Act in 2005 based on the state's legal battles with the inmate. This act was struck down in 2010 as unconstitutional not only because it "amount[ed] to deliberate indifference to . . . serious medical needs" but also because it was found to violate rights to equal protection (Cohen, 2011, p. 49; see also Vielmetti, 2012). While Konitzer accepted a settlement from the state in 2010 for a lawsuit she filed in 2003, just weeks later she asked that the settlement be thrown out due to coercion during the process and her desire to continue to fight for the option of sex reassignment surgery (Foley, 2010). Interestingly, one request the state had originally denied was Konitzer's request to wear women's undergarments. Prison authorities contended that wearing these undergarments would increase her risk for victimization.

While courts have recognized the need for medical treatment, especially for the continuation of hormone therapy, a great deal of controversy surrounds the topic of such treatment for gender identity disorder. This disagreement is exacerbated when the state is made responsible for providing the treatment for transgender inmates. Some contend that since the disorder is psychological, and not medical, medical treatments are not appropriate (Richey, 2012). Another argument against sex reassignment surgery for inmates is that eligibility may raise the crime rate among the transgendered population. Transgendered individuals may see being in prison as a way to have the surgery without paying for it (Barton, 2005). Whether or not this concern is realistic, the above-discussed cases go to show that courts have continued to reject states' attempts to not provide such treatment to transgendered inmates.

Management of Transgender Inmates

While transgender inmates challenge the status quo, research has found that a majority of corrections departments do not have formal policies for the management of transgender inmates. One international study in particular found that only 20 percent of corrections departments participating in the study had formal policies, while another 20 percent had informal policies related to the treatment and housing of these inmates (Petersen et al., 1996). Without formal policies governing a population that is overrepresented in prison (Tarzwell, 2006), issues such as those discussed above are bound to arise. To combat this, Leach (2007) contends prison and jail administrators have to question their entire process from intake to classification, to housing, to treatment (see Table 6.2). Tarzwell (2006) also provides a number of policy suggestions including (1) inclusion of transgender individuals and advocates in the policymaking process; (2) development of

Table 6.2 Managing Transsexual Inmates

Questions posed in the management of transsexual inmates:

1. What different medical and mental health services must we provide to transsexual offenders?
2. Is there a need for a greater level of service and support for the sexual reassignment process?
3. What is the psychological impact of impeding the sexual reassignment process?
4. Does this rise to the level of "serious medical need"?
5. Who makes the determination of this "serious medical need"?
6. Do we book this person in our management information systems as a male or a female?
7. Do we make changes to that information once the surgical procedures are completed?
8. What is the basis for determining designation of "sex"? What does being a transsexual and having a "gender identity" do to this determination?
9. Do we have to perform cavity searches differently based on being a transsexual or gender identity?
10. Do we have to house transsexual inmates outside general population cell blocks?

Source: Leach (2007, pp. 78–79).

a "management and treatment plan" for each transgender inmate by a transgender committee; (3) basing placement decisions on "the prisoner's subjective gender identity, placement preference, and safety" (p. 213); (4) determination of "gender-affirming medical care" by a transgender committee with inmate input (p. 214); and (5) intake screening for transgender identity and vulnerability based on self-identification.

In most prisons and jails transgender inmates can be found among the general population unless a specific risk is identified. Instances of correctional housing units reserved for vulnerable inmates can be found. Some correctional authorities, in addition, have made the decision to segregate not only transgender inmates but also inmates self-identifying as gay. The K6G Unit of Los Angeles County Men's Central Jail represents such a practice. K6G is a housing unit for gay males and transwomen who self-identify during the intake process. While on its face it may look like the Los Angeles County Men's Central Jail is doing what it can to protect these inmates, Robinson (2011) contends that K6G is a "clever decoy" (p. 1314), pointing out that jail administrators are, in fact, not following the recommendations of the Prison Rape Elimination Act. Instead, classification is based on sexual orientation and transgender orientation only. No consideration is given to other factors that increase vulnerability among the male inmate population. Therefore, many inmates who are in fact vulnerable may not be considered for the unit if they do not self-identify as a gay male or transfemale during the intake process. Los Angeles County Men's Central Jail is not the only correctional complex where such segregation has been attempted. Correctional authorities at Rikers Island also followed such a practice until 2005 (Von Zielauer, 2005). Similar to the jail in Los Angeles County, if inmates self-identified as gay or transgender or were visibly transgender, they would be segregated in a special unit. Because classification was based on self-identification, however, inmate predators were found to lie in order to access the unit where they could exploit weak inmates. Subsequently, Rikers Island officials decided to close the unit and instead house vulnerable inmates who ask for protective custody in a similar fashion to solitary confinement for which gay and transgender inmates would be locked down for twenty-three hours a day. As these two examples show, room still exists for improvement in protective segregation for transgender and other vulnerable inmates. Lockdown confinement is not preferred, but neither is the possibility that predators will obtain open access to a supposedly protective housing unit.

Transgender inmates need special attention when confined in a jail or prison as these inmates are at a higher risk for victimization, especially sexual victimization. Not only are these inmates at risk from other inmates, but they may also be at risk for having their rights violated by prison authorities. Inmates and correctional officials alike need written formal policies and equitable procedures, which are followed when classifying inmates, determining safe placement, and making decisions regarding medical treatment. Until these issues are resolved, managing this special inmate population will remain a challenge for prison officials.

Conclusion

Sexuality is fluid. Inmates entering prison with one sexual orientation or sexual identity may modify one, the other, or both during their sentence (Garland, Morgan, and Beer, 2005; Hensley, Tewksbury, and Wright, 2001; Kocheski and Hensley, 2001). This fluidity suggests that the process of identifying who is homosexual, bisexual, and transgendered in prison takes place in a highly contextualized moment, dependent on a variety of factors (Garland, Morgan, and Beer, 2005). Processes of using sexual behavior to categorize inmates' sexuality may run afoul as their sexual identities and orientations may not be congruent with their behavior. For instance, nonaggressive "wolves" view themselves as heterosexuals but openly engage in same-sex relations with inmates acting out feminine homosexual roles. For this same reason, counts of same-sex sexual behavior are routinely higher than those of orientation or identity. What can be assessed are individuals' current and preprison sexualities. Prison scholars can compare these in an effort to gain knowledge about the stability and change in sexuality across individuals' sentences. Inmates use the preprison characteristics to inform them on how a person may fit in to the prison sex scene. What we see is how inmates rely on preprison dimensions of sexuality and use them to pressure inmates into sociosexual roles, pressuring male inmates into feminine homosexual roles of "queens," "punks," and "true homosexuals" (Fleisher and Krienert, 2009; Wooden and Parker, 1982). To be fair, inmates use other nonsexual criteria to also determine who may or may not be pressured into particular feminine sex roles, as well (Nacci and Kane, 1984b).

Interestingly, despite the fluidity of sexuality, male and female inmates in sex-segregated prison environments subscribe to prison sexual subcultural tenets based on free-community gender roles. Female prison sexual culture creates masculine roles for women to fill (Giallombardo, 1966; Owen, 1998). Some male inmates take on culturally defined feminine roles (Clemmer, 1958, Wooden and Parker, 1982). While inmates import these prison gendered roles from mainstream culture, the way that these are adapted are based on the divergent natures of male and female prison environments. Women inmates tend to form pseudofamilies to adapt to the pains of imprisonment (Heffernan, 1972; R. S. Jones, 1993; Owen, 1998), adopting gendered kinship roles. These relationships can be homosexual for some members and platonic for others, stressing the importance of the emotional support needed to endure prison (Giallombardo, 1966; R. S. Jones, 1993; Propper, 1982).

What are prisons to do, if anything, in managing risk and harm for nonheterosexual inmates? Nacci and Kane (1984b) offer the point that to reduce sexual violence, concomitant reduction in same-sex sexual behavior is also required. As such, they advise against the use of segregated environments for those members of prison. What is more commonplace is segregation based on risk reduction. This segregation may take the form of individual protective custody where individuals are locked away most hours of the day or where groups of targeted individuals reside under custody with one another. Potential problems associated with these special housing units involve misclassification such that a target is placed in a perpetrator-rich environment, or vice versa, a perpetrator is placed in a target-rich environment, resulting in greater harm. Additionally, Alarid (2000b) reported the phenomenon where targets of sexual violence began to pressure other targeted inmates.

While administrators work to uncover the best practices, researchers should remain persistent in their study of the prison sexual culture. New findings can be used to modify or discard existing models on what we believe to be true of how sex and sexuality intersect with prison life. These research endeavors should be used to gain knowledge that informs policy and practice for a diverse, tolerant, and less coercive prison environment for all inmates.

7

Health Issues

Roberto Hugh Potter and Jeffrey Rosky

At the end of the twentieth century, Tewksbury and West (2000) wrote that researching sexual behavior among inmates and prisoners was a risky strategy for young, tenure-seeking social science faculty. They reviewed the relatively scarce social science base that existed on the topic by the late 1990s. The same caveat apparently did not apply to researchers in the public health and medical epidemiology domains when it came to studying the incidence and prevalence of STDs among correctional populations. Since at least the recognition of AIDS and other STDs as epidemic, public health epidemiologists had been reporting on such diseases, especially among jail populations. This information was rarely presented in criminology and criminal justice journals, however.

Moving beyond security issues, one of the most frequently cited concerns about sexual behavior in correctional settings focuses on the spread of infectious diseases, many of which become chronic conditions and are potentially fatal. Among the areas Tewksbury and West (2000) list as important in studying sexual behavior in prisons are "health problems related to sexual activities" (p. 173) and the implications these problems have for the inmates, staff, and the general public along with the unfortunate association that sex in prisons has with violence (Potter and Tewksbury, 2005).

Sexual behaviors and health outcomes in correctional facilities pose several issues for the management, line personnel, and inmates of the facilities including

- Identification of infectious diseases among those who enter the facility.
- Prevention of the transmission of such diseases among the occupants of the facilities and to the staff of the facility.
- Maintenance of the "good order" of the facility in terms of violence that might be associated with sexual networks in the facility.
- Treatment of STDs and blood-borne infections imported into or acquired within the facility.
- Cultivation of linkages to services in the community following release to treat inmates with those diseases that require postincarceration continuity of care.

In addressing these concerns, we examine them in light of the concepts of importation and deprivation (Clemmer, 1940) and how they relate to transmission of sexually acquired diseases within correctional facilities. But dealing with health issues inside prisons is only part of the equation, and to truly understand the big picture, we must also examine exportation from the corrections environment to the community to understand fully why sex, disease, and corrections seem to pose problems to criminal justice and public health professionals alike.

What Comes Through the Door:
Community Lifestyles and Disease Importation
Screening and Treatment

Generally speaking, the incidence of sexually transmitted diseases observed in correctional populations, especially in jails, is significantly higher than observed in the community (Williams and Kahn, 2007). Williams and Kahn (2007) summarized the published reports in the first six months of 2001:

• Chlamydia: 14–20 percent in female adolescent detainees; 7–12 percent in male adolescent detainees; 7.2 percent (range, 1.2–22.7

percent) in adult females entering 32 corrections facilities; 10.2 percent (range, 0.7–30.0 percent) for adult males entering 35 corrections facilities (Williams and Kahn, 2007, p. 376).

• Gonorrhea: median 4.5 percent (range, 0–16.6 percent) in female adolescent detainees (34 facilities); median 3.0 percent (range, 0–8.4 percent) positivity for adult females (26 facilities); median 0.8 percent (range, 0–18.2 percent) among adolescent males (49 facilities); median 2.6 percent (range, 0–33.8 percent) for adult males (27 facilities) (Williams and Kahn, 2007, pp. 376–377).

• Syphilis: in general, more prevalent among incarcerated women (5.3 percent; range, 0–19 percent) than men (2.7 percent; range, 0.2–5.9 percent), and more prevalent in persons admitted to jails than juvenile facilities (Williams and Kahn, 2007, p. 377).

Kahn and colleagues (Kahn et al., 2002; Kahn et al., 2004) reported testing results from thirty US jails selected because of high syphilis morbidity in their communities, not because they were representative of US jails. Chen, Bovée, and Kerndt (2003), for example, reported syphilis-screening results from 811 inmates from the Los Angeles County jail, which held around 20,000 inmates on any given day during the year of the testing program. All of those tested in the report were housed in a special unit for self-identified gay or transgendered inmates.

Potter and colleagues (2011) provided a table of published studies of disease, injury, and mental health screenings conducted in jail and prison settings through 2009 that included STD/HIV screening. Among the issues they raised was representativeness of these data. Published studies of STDs among correctional populations are not drawn from representative samples of jails and prisons and are often focused on a single facility.

We must point out that the "significantly higher rates of STDs than observed in the general community" statements that generally accompany such descriptive epidemiological studies obscure the reality that jail and prison populations are not drawn from the general community. Correctional populations are disproportionately drawn from poor and minority communities. Not surprisingly, rates of STDs in the community demonstrate similar disproportional impact on minority communities, especially among African Americans. The data presented in Table 7.1 show that disproportionate rates of disease

Table 7.1 Rate (per 100,000 population) of Selected Sexually Transmitted Diseases by Racial Groups, 2005–2011

Year	Chlamydia		Gonorrhea		Syphilis		HIV/AIDS	
	White	African-American	White	African-American	White	African-American	White	African-American
2005	151.7	1,234.3	35.1	619.4	1.8	9.7	6.9	68.7
2006	153.1	1,275.0	36.5	658.4	1.9	11.3	6.4	60.3
2007	118.1	1,015.7	27.0	515.2	1.9	13.2	7.7	62.0
2008	125.0	1,100.6	24.1	489.0	2.1	16.6	7.3	63.2
2009	129.2	1,122.2	21.1	431.1	2.0	18.4	6.9	59.8
2010	140.1	1,150.4	23.4	426.2	2.1	16.6	7.3	62.0
2011	159.0	1,194.4	25.2	427.3	2.3	15.5	7.0	60.4

Sources: Centers for Disease Control and Prvention (2005, 2008, 2011, 2012); US Department of Health and Human Services (2007, 2011, 2012).

in the African American community may help explain some of the higher rates in the correctional setting. Unfortunately, we are not comparing similar fruit here, as STD studies are much less representative of the nation than are the disease rates. When taking into account specific behaviors occurring among these groups while in the free community, some of which are criminal (e.g., injection drug use, prostitution), the disproportionality of STDs observed in correctional settings should not be terribly shocking.

Indeed, Marquart and colleagues (1996) have explored the relationships among community health factors and correctional health issues. Their analysis provided support for Harts's inverse care law (Hart, 1971), which argues that those who most need access to care are often in communities where such care is either nonexistent or below the level needed. Williams and Kahn acknowledged this fact: "The considerable prevalence of STDs/HIV in communities coaffected by high rates of incarceration (and the associated factors) is indicative of a failed societal effort to devise healthy communities and inhibit criminogenic motivations, as well as a failed public health effort to facilitate health care access and acquisition of optimal health" (Williams and Kahn, 2007, p. 375).

Table 7.2 provides another way of examining the relationship between health burden in a community and impact on minority communities. The inmate data in Table 7.2 were compiled from Bureau of Justice Statistics reports on jail inmate counts at midyear 2004 (Har-

Table 7.2 Comparison of 2004 Metropolitan Statistical Area (MSA) Population and Jail Population with Rate of AIDS (per 100,000 population), Syphilis, and Hepatitis Morbidity Rate (per 100,000 population) in the Twenty-five Largest Jails in the United States

Jail Population Rank[a]	County, City[a]	Population[a]	Jail Population[a]	AIDS Case Rate[b]	Syphillis High Morbidity Area,[c] Yes or No	Hepatitis B Rate[c]
1	Los Angeles County	9,937,739	19,732	20.8	Y	0.9
2	New York City	8,085,742	13,153	41.9	Y	2.0
3	Cook County, Chicago	5,327,777	9,872	17.8	Y	1.1
4	Maricopa County, Phoenix	3,501,001	9,584	11.6	Y	5.1
5	Harris County, Houston	3,644,285	9,031	23.9	Y	4.5
6	Philadelphia	1,470,151	7,769	26.6	Y	4.1
7	Dallas County	2,294,706	7,392	19.2	Y	3.0
8	Miami-Dade County	1,101,261	6,558	45.2	Y	5.4
9	Orange County, Anaheim	2,987,591	6,493	n.a.	N	1.0
10	New Orleans Parish	462,269	6,295	31.9	Y	4.1
11	San Bernardino County	1,921,131	5,753	n.a.	N	0.7
12	Broward County, Ft. Lauderdale	1,754,893	5,395	58.4	N	3.8
13	San Diego County	2,931,714	5,039	n.a.	N	0.4
14	Hillsborough County, Tampa	821,338	4,729	25.7	Y	4.0
15	Santa Clara County	1,685,188	4,566	n.a.	Y	0.4
16	Bexar County, San Antonio	1,493,965	4,109	n.a.	Y	7.5

(continues)

118

Table 7.2 continued

Jail Population Rank[a]	County, City[a]	Population[a]	Jail Population[a]	AIDS Case Rate[b]	Syphillis High Morbidity Area,[c] Yes or No	Hepatitis B Rate[c]
17	Alameda County, Oakland	1,455,235	4,083	12.3	N	0.1
18	Sacramento County	1,352,445	3,985	4.3	N	0.7
19	Orange County, Orlando	989,926	3,735	31.2	N	4.7
20	Pinellas County, St. Pete	928,537	3,600	25.7	Y	5.2
21	Jacksonville-Duval County					
22	Washington, DC, Department of Corrections	2,363,600	3,580	29.9	Y	1.8
		553,523	3,552	40.3	Y	3.4
23	Baltimore City	780,821	3,490	32.8	Y	6.8
24	Tarrant County, Ft. Worth TX	1,588,088	3,393	9.9	N	1.8
25	Fulton County, Atlanta metro	814,438	3,202	21.5	Y	9.8

Sources: a. Beck and Harrison (2003).
b. Personal Communication (2005), Division of HIV/AIDS Prevention (Robin MacGowan).
c. Division of STD Prevention and Control (Norman Fikes).
d. Division of Viral Hepatitis (Cindy Weinberg), Centers for Disease Control and Prevention.

rison and Beck, 2003) for the twenty-five largest county jail facilities. The county-level reported AIDS (not HIV) case rates were obtained from the Division of HIV/AIDS Prevention, the syphilis morbidity data from the Division of STD Prevention and Control, and the acute hepatitis B rates from the Division of Viral Hepatitis at the Centers for Disease Control and Prevention when one of the authors of this chapter was employed there. All of the diseases are transmitted sexually or through blood or both. The data presented demonstrate a correspondence in many larger communities between the size of the jail population and the levels of infectious diseases observed in the community. Because the community rates of disease are high, little reason can be found to believe they would not be at least reflected in the disease burden among inmates, if not sharpened by the socioeconomic filtering that occurs with jail populations.

Potter and colleagues (2011) also examined the point at which testing occurred across the studies of HIV and STD screening. For the STD studies, such data were often not reported. Most studies reported testing within the first seventy-two hours of entry into a jail or prison facility. Potter and colleagues' conclusion was that most of our knowledge about the STD and HIV disease burden among correctional populations is drawn at the front end of the process, at which point most people will be reentering the community within forty-eight to seventy-two hours. The STDs that are brought into the facility are likely to return to the community in relatively short order. Regrettably, almost as many cases of disease are likely to be untreated when these individuals leave jails as they were when they arrived. Due to the short amount of time of incarceration and the lack of resources to complete testing and treatment on all inmates, we are not able to diagnose and treat inmates ideally before release.

What Happens Inside? Factors Associated with Correctional STD Transmission

"If it can happen in the free world, it can happen inside; but generally at a reduced frequency" (Potter, 2007, p. 43) is one way of addressing the reality that sex (and other exchanges of bodily fluids) occur within correctional facilities. Two of the first "facts" to be determined in discussing STD transmission in correctional facilities are the prevalence of sexually transmitted diseases among the incarcerated population and the prevalence and frequency of sexual behavior among incarcerated persons. In epidemiological terms, these are the "denominator" figures of "how much" and "how often" necessary to begin making empirical statements about STD transmission in correctional facilities.

As the reader might expect, figuring out how much STD there is and how often inmates have sex is no easy task. As noted earlier, most people passing through jails in the United States are unlikely to spend enough time there to submit to an STD test and receive results, initiate treatment, and arrange for community follow-up treatment. Prison facilities should provide a much more stable environment in which to conduct STD screening and initiate treatment.

Surveillance

As noted elsewhere (Potter and Krider, 2000), public health agencies use the term *surveillance* in roughly the same way that criminal justice agencies use the term *monitoring* in relation to recorded events. Public health surveillance is defined by the World Health Organization (2007) as "the continuous, systematic collection, analysis and interpretation of health-related data needed for the planning, implementation, and evaluation of public health practice." Health surveillance systems establish base rates of disease data in order to observe when a deviation from the endemic becomes epidemic, or a disease has been eliminated. If the base rate of a disease is zero, then any newly observed case of the disease is an "outbreak" in surveillance terms.

To establish base rates of disease in a correctional system requires that testing for the particular disease be carried out on a continuous systematic basis. This testing is much more likely to occur in prisons than it is in the vast majority of jails due to a combination of size and detainee flow among jails. However, once that base rate is established, then deviations from the base rate will allow us to discuss the transmission of disease within correctional facilities with much greater confidence. As discussed in Potter and colleagues (2011), however, most studies of STD/HIV "outbreaks" in correctional facilities assume a base rate of zero, so any transmission of the disease is considered a significant event.

Akers, Potter, and Hill (2013) provide an overview of the primary techniques for monitoring disease utilized to date in studies conducted among correctional populations. These include "serostatus" studies in which blood is drawn or a cheek swab is taken from inmates and prisoners upon entry and at exit. Any difference between disease status at exit from the entry test provides evidence of disease transmission. Alternatively, some studies have utilized pharmacy records and International Classification of Disease codes to observe changes in health status among prisoners over time in prison to infer disease transmission. We will refer the reader to the longer discussion of the strengths and weaknesses of these and other techniques for monitoring diseases in correctional facilities in Akers, Potter, and Hill (2013).

As noted above, disease transmission is possible within correctional facilities, just as any other phenomenon is possible, but probably occurs at a lower rate than observed in the free community. The rare event is interesting to academics, but unlikely to provide much assistance to the correctional administrator in terms of reducing the likelihood of the rare event. Thus, studies of "one-off" events of disease transmission in correctional facilities are interesting, but they do little to assist us in the prevention of such rare events. Our attention is probably best directed toward identifying treatable STDs and providing treatment early in the jail or prison stay. Likewise, for those STDs such as HIV and viral hepatitis that become chronic conditions, early intervention and treatment initiation can provide reduced viral loads and likelihood of transmission when behavioral interventions to reduce opportunity for disease transmission fail.

Here again we encounter the draw of the unique versus the reality of the mundane. One of the authors of this chapter, testifying at a Prison Rape Elimination Commission hearing, had the experience of following a panel of survivors of prison rape, one of whom testified he had contracted HIV as a result of sexual assault while incarcerated. Following that testimony with a presentation on how no published literature existed on sustained and substantiated HIV transmission as a result of rape in prisons was an uncomfortable situation. Acknowledging that the lived experiences of individuals and the requirements of published social science are quite different seemed to satisfy the hearing participants.

Screening

To establish disease transmission, then, we must have entry and exit tests. In addition to the point at which STD and HIV testing occurred, as noted earlier, Potter and colleagues (2011) also summarized the "burden" of disease found among participants in various jails and prisons in the published literature to 2009. Burden was generally expressed as the percentage of the population tested whose results were positive for the disease or diseases assessed. In some instances these results were reported as the percentage of all cases of the disease reported in the city or county during the time frame covered by testing in the jail. Only two of the studies included more than one jail system, one with jails in four states and another with jails in thirty counties with high syphilis morbidity. The number of detainees tested ranged from 27 to more than 50,000 in one multistate, multiyear project.

The first point to be made is that we have relatively little published data from state prison systems and about a 1 percent sample of jails in the United States for which we can make statements about STD and HIV transmission in correctional facilities. More testing is done at prison levels than is reported in the academic literature, to be sure. Every state correctional system conducts a full physical examination, including blood work, on new entrants to their facilities within the first two weeks of incarceration. Maruschak (2009) has published information on HIV testing procedures, and a more specific set of questions is planned for future use. Whether testing for HIV and other STDs is voluntary or mandatory or only occurs when medical staff think it is indicated is a key issue in having confidence in the levels of disease identified at the intake point. If all such testing is voluntary, and someone refuses testing, then determining whether subsequent positive tests for an STD or HIV are the result of intrafacility transmission or were brought into the facility but unrecognized on initial examination is difficult (but not necessarily impossible).

Since AIDS became a recognized problem in correctional facilities, several studies have examined HIV transmission within prisons, with many more documenting risk behaviors such as sex (consensual and nonconsensual), injection drug use, and tattooing that occur in prisons and might lead to HIV transmission. Brewer and colleagues (1988) examined blood samples (serosamples) taken from inmates at intake to an eastern state prison system and within two years of entry for those who remained and consented, or 422 of an original 2,286 prisoner sample. They documented two cases of seroconversion (became HIV positive), both of whom had been incarcerated for fewer than six months. Horsburgh and colleagues (1990) examined serosamples among all entering prisoners in a small western prison system and again at two and three years' postentry. They found two prisoners had seroconverted with high likelihood of in-facility acquisition, and one prisoner possibly infected inside, but within the six-month "window" period, which could indicate infection occurred prior to incarceration.

Krebs (Krebs, 2006; Krebs and Simmons, 2002) documented thirty-three cases of HIV transmission in a large southern prison system over the course of twenty-two years using medical history data. His data allowed for a six-month "window" period for the HIV to manifest given the testing technology of the period. That is, prisoners whose HIV was diagnosed earlier than six months into their incarceration period were counted as being possibly infected prior to arrival at prison. Jafa and colleagues (2009) examined eighty-eight documented cases of seroconversion among males within an adjacent large southern prison system between 1988 and 2005. Nearly half of the documented cases (forty-one, or 47 percent) occurred between 2003 and 2005 when HIV testing was offered at prisoners' annual physical examinations, a practice curtailed for cost-cutting reasons shortly thereafter. In a 2006 exchange between the medical director and the clinical services director at the time of the investigation, the discussion of exactly how "large" such figures were was raised. In absolute terms, the findings represented a rate of about 5.1 transmissions per 50,000 inmates during the two years with the best data; an argument was also presented that without a follow-up test for those who discharged without such a test, computing a rough rate was not useful (Paris and LaMarre, 2006).

Little disagreement should exist that HIV, other STDs, and viral hepatitis (A, B, and C) are transmitted in correctional facilities. However, the exact rate of transmission of HIV or any STD or blood-borne disease is unlikely to be known because of turnover in staff and measurement techniques. This inaccuracy is especially true for jails whose rapid "flow" and annual turnover are much greater than those of prisons. Even if Dr. Paris's estimate of 0.001 percent annually is true, the seventy-five individuals infected annually will themselves experience significant impacts, as will the correctional systems and the communities. Every case of new HIV is going to cost the state government at least $10,000 annually added to the general cost of maintaining a prisoner in the system. The lifelong impact on the prisoner and his or her social support network is significant, even if we can't put a dollar value on it.

Not all sexually transmitted and blood-borne infections are acquired through sexual behaviors, of course. In the study by Jafa and colleagues (2009), tattooing was among the "risk behaviors" that demonstrated a statistically significant relationship to seroconversion in the men in the 2003–2005 group. Injection drug use and needle sharing are behaviors that have been both documented and suggested as risk behaviors in other studies (Kang et al., 2005). In just about all jail and prison systems, sexual behaviors—regardless of consent—are included among prohibited behaviors subject to organizational sanctions. Prevention and reaction activities to reduce or eliminate such behaviors in correctional facilities often present areas of disagreement between correctional and public health officials. We will return to this point later.

Treatment

Once an illness is identified in a correctional facility, the person living with the illness has the legal right to be treated for the disease. Anno (1991) noted that incarcerated individuals have the right to competent medical care as ordered by a medical professional. Correctional institutions themselves have an interest in addressing infectious diseases to reduce transmission and expand treatment in the facility. As well, correctional institutions have an interest in the efficient management of chronic diseases to reduce the long-term costs associated with disease progression. For example, keeping the HIV viral load low in a person living with HIV reduces opportunistic infections and general health decline that might cost the institution more than ongoing treatment for the disease.

For bacterial STDs, a range of antibiotic treatments, many relatively low cost, are available to cure the diseases. Some bacterial STDs, notably gonorrhea, are developing resistance to existing treatments and represent a potential treatment challenge. Viral STDs, such as the range of hepatitis infections and HIV, require more sophisticated antiretroviral treatments, which bear substantial costs. In fact, HIV and hepatitis C treatments represent a substantial proportion of some correctional facilities' health-care budgets, on a par with psychotropic medications. Notably, many more people are on psychotropic medications than people living with HIV or active hepatitis C in most facilities. Thus, STDs and blood-borne infections represent a substantial health-care burden for institutions, regardless of where the disease was contracted.

Transition to the Community

We noted earlier that we really need exit testing for diseases to understand what health-care burden leaves the correctional facility and whether it was brought into the facility from the community or contracted in the facility itself. The reality is that, other than select diseases such as HIV, unless an inmate or prisoner requires continuity of care when returning to the community for a known disease, we have little information about how much disease returns to the community. The existing knowledge is contained primarily in medical records and rarely published.

Different Perceptions, Different Responses

To recap, sexual behaviors and health outcomes in correctional facilities pose several issues for the management, line personnel, and inmates of the facilities. First among these is the identification of infectious diseases among those who enter the facility. Next is the issue of preventing the transmission of such diseases among the occupants of the facilities and, on occasion, to the staff of the facility. Mixed in here are issues of maintenance of the "good order" of the facility in terms of violence that might be associated with sexual networks in the facility. Treatment of STDs and blood-borne infections brought from the outside or acquired in the facility is another area of concern, as is linkage to services in the community following release for those diseases that were not cured during the period of incarceration.

We have argued that the precise burden of STDs and blood-borne infections that enter jails is unlikely to be known; however, in prisons such infections will more likely be identified and treatment initiated at intake. Those diseases that are chronic, but infectious, pose particular challenges for correctional administrators in terms of the prevention of transmission. These break down essentially into two categories: deterrence versus public health approaches.

Potter and Krider (2000), as well as Potter and Rosky (2013), have examined the differences between deterrence-based and public health approaches to the prevention of inappropriate sexual behavior, in particular. Here we want to focus on the difference in prohibition and deterrence-based programs generally practiced in correctional facilities and the "harm reduction" approaches favored generally by public health practitioners. Both of these perspectives are grounded in the belief that sexual behaviors (as well as substance use and tattooing) will occur in correctional settings. After all, many if not most of the people who find themselves as guests of the state for criminal activities have difficulty following rules. Even though everyone who goes through a classification process at a larger jail and prison will receive a copy of the rules of behavior for the facility, it does not mean they will follow those rules religiously.

Standard correctional practice partially involves what Sykes (1958) termed the "pains of imprisonment." In Sykes's analysis, prisoners faced key "deprivations" when incarcerated. These included deprivation of liberty, deprivation of goods and services, deprivation of heterosexual relations, deprivation of autonomy, and deprivation of security. While strides have been made to shore up the security aspects of jail and prison life (e.g., the Prison Rape Elimination Act [PREA]), the three remaining deprivations characterize the incarceration experience for many. Part of enhancing the security aspects of carceral life includes the prohibition of activities such as sexual behavior. Sex does become a commodity in prisons (Fleisher and Krienert, 2009), and limiting its availability may make it an even more desired commodity. To overcome this, the deterrent idea of the punishment outweighing the risk is a key to preventing the unwanted behavior. Certainty and swiftness of proportional punishment is the follow-up for breaking the rule. Hypothetically, a rational inmate will calculate the risk and decide the punishment is too great, reducing the likelihood of committing the prohibited behavior.

On the other hand, public health advocates begin from the perspective that sex (like substance use and tattooing) in correctional facilities is inevitable. Rather than trying to use deterrent techniques to prevent it, they accept that it will happen and reduce the harms associated with it. This "harm reduction" (Kerr et al., 2004) approach leads to suggestions that, in order to reduce the health harms associated with sexual behavior in correctional facilities, correctional officials should distribute condoms to prisoners (as well as clean needles, syringes, and so on). Since no one can stop the behaviors, administrators should minimize the possible health risks associated with them, regardless of whether these harm reduction techniques violate facility, agency, state, or federal laws or policies. And, to be clear, in the United States, such materials are defined as contraband in almost every correctional facility.

The reader will no doubt sense some tension between these two approaches. We should note that some prison and jail systems in the United States, some prisons in Australian states, and some in European countries provide some or all of these materials to inmates. Generally speaking, the more inappropriate and potentially dangerous uses of condoms—such as being filled with sand to create an impromptu blackjack—have not materialized where condoms have been introduced. Other aspects of "good order" in the facility have not been rigorously studied so far.

Here lies one of the thorniest topics with regard to how we approach the issue of sexual relations in correctional facilities and the related health impacts. Do we continue to rely on our deterrence-, rules-based disciplinary regimes to keep the rates of disease transmission (and violence-related injuries) relatively low? Or do we accept the "inevitable" and provide materials such as condoms and lubricant to the inmates in the hope they will utilize them? Perhaps there is a third path we can explore that maintains good order in our facilities while reducing the already low health impact of the sex that does occur on the inside? We rely on the next generation of correctional professionals to explore these thorny options.

Conclusion

We have examined the issue of sexual behavior in correctional facilities from a focus on sexually transmitted and blood-borne diseases such as a range of bacterial STDs and viral diseases such as HIV and the range of hepatitis infections. We established the need to distinguish between the burden of disease that enters correctional facilities, the disease transmitted among the incarcerated, and the disease that reenters the community upon discharge. We noted that, other than a handful of funded academic publications, most correctional health data are not published. Thus, we have little broad knowledge of the true burden of sexually transmitted and blood-borne diseases available, especially since the beginning of the twenty-first century.

Sex does occur inside correctional facilities, and it has been shown that some disease transmission does occur as a result of this behavior. In most correctional facilities in the United States, sexual behavior, and some disease prevention measures (e.g., condoms), are against the rules of the institutions. Whether we respond with traditional prohibitive polices or turn to a more "harm reduction" approach to such behaviors is a question with which future correctional and health leaders will grapple.

We also demonstrated that disease rates in correctional systems reflect the disease burden in the communities served by those correctional systems. The success or failure of public health disease prevention efforts in communities directly determines the burden of disease that will enter a correctional facility. The role of correctional facilities, especially jails, in the detection and management of community-acquired STDs, HIV, and hepatitis within the legal and operational requirements of those facilities remains an area of debate. The same is true of the impact on communities once individuals living with viral infections and untreated bacterial infections return to the community. Coming to useful conclusions through these debates will require future correctional leaders to engage with public health leadership to examine ways corrections can effectively and efficiently play a role in maintaining the health of the community.

The transmission of disease through sexual contact in correctional facilities does have a potentially negative impact on those facilities, an impact that is particularly vivid in terms of the cost of treating many viral, chronic STDs. Whether this impact is greater than the potential disruptions to the "good order" of a facility as the result of sexual jealousy and violence remains an open question.

8

International Contexts

Tomer Einat

Deprivation of basic human needs and the search for alternative sources of gratification are the forces that shape the world of the prison—its values, way of life, and the roles of those trapped within it. In a culture that places the quest for power and dominance at the forefront, male inmates are deprived of heterosexual relationships and stripped of various traditional means of asserting their masculinity (Einat and Einat, 2000; Sykes, 1958; Toch, 1992). All this creates "extreme emotional, psychological, and perhaps physical distress" (Tewksbury and West, 2000, p. 369), which drives many male inmates to engage in same-sex sexual activities with consenting or coerced partners, thus reestablishing their sense of dominance, respect, and self-esteem (Dumond, 2000; Hensley, 2001; Man and Cronan, 2002).

Research on consensual or coerced same-sex sexual relations in non-US male correctional facilities has been sparse (Awofeso and Naoum, 2002; Green et al., 2003), and has yielded inconsistent findings. Richters and colleagues (2012) conducted a computer-assisted telephone interview survey of a random sample of 2,089 male prisoners in New South Wales and Queensland, as part of the Sexual Health and Attitudes of Australian Prisoners Study. Generally, the inmates were asked several different questions about sexual contact with other inmates in prison and about sexual coercion. The study revealed that 7.1 percent of the total sample reported sexual contact with inmates in prison, be it for pleasure or protection. In addition, 6.9 percent of the total sample reported being sexually threatened in prison and 2.6 percent reported being sexually coerced.

In parallel research that was part of the above study as well, Yap and colleagues (2011) analyzed the decline in sexual assaults in men's prisons in New South Wales between the years 1996 and 2009. Thirty-three men and seven male-to-female transgendered people who had served or were currently serving sentences in a New South Wales prison were asked about same-sex sexual assaults in prison, sexual networks in jail, sex in exchange for goods and favors, sex inside and outside prison, and sexual meanings. Qualitative analysis of the data revealed a convergence of historical events and policy changes from the mid-1990s and on. Namely, reduction of the number of prisoners in each cell, assumption of legal responsibility for the safety of the inmates by the state, introduction of new video surveillance and recording equipment, and imposition of stricter supervision and discipline by prison authorities on the prison's own custodial staff were the main factors for such decline.

A third Australian study (Yap et al., 2007) examined the long-term effects of the introduction of condoms and dental dams into New South Wales prisons, focusing on four particular concerns raised by politicians, prison officers, prison nurses, and prisoners: (1) condoms would encourage inmates to have same-sex sexual relationships in prison, (2) condoms would lead to an increase in sexual assaults in prison, (3) prisoners would use condoms to hide and store drugs and other contraband, and (4) prisoners would use condoms as weapons. A random sample of 747 inmates from twenty-nine prison facilities were asked about their experiences of consensual and nonconsensual same-sex sexual relations in prison and their own use of condoms or dental dams for sexual purposes (in addition to questions relating to other nonsexual uses of condoms). The researchers discovered a decrease in reports of both consensual (6.3 percent, down to 2.4 percent) and nonconsensual (2.6 percent, down to 0.3 percent) same-sex sexual relations among men five years after the introduction of condoms into prisons.

In England and Wales, Green and colleagues (2003) conducted a two-year study of 1,009 adult male prisoners from thirteen prisons about sexual behavior, drug use, and tattooing, inside and outside of prison. The study revealed that overall, between 2.2 percent (n = 22) and 2.4 percent (n = 24) of the random sample reported having same-sex sexual activity in prison. Furthermore, six of the men who reported engaging in same-sex sexual activity in prison said that they had been pressured at one time or another. Interestingly, two of the twenty-two men who reported engaging in same-sex sexual activity while in prison reported that it was their first same-sex sexual experience. For both men, sex was consensual. A simultaneous study, conducted by Edgar, O'Donnell, and Martin (2003), revealed that of 590 prisoners interviewed in various English penal institutions, less than 2 percent said they had been sexually attacked while in custody.

A national survey of the prevalence of HIV, hepatitis B, and hepatitis C antibodies in prisoners in England and Wales in the year 2000 revealed that only 3.5 percent of the adult male participants (n = 92) and 0.4 percent of male young prisoners (n = 3) had ever had anal sex inside prison (Weild et al., 2000).

Power and colleagues (1991) interviewed 559 (11.7 percent of the total Scottish prison population) male and female remand, short-term and long-term inmates, randomly allocated from eight penal establishments, with regard to their same-sex sexual behavior in prison, intravenous drug use, and knowledge and attitudes with respect to HIV and AIDS. The findings of the study revealed that only one male inmate and three female prisoners reported being same-sex sexually active during the period of their incarceration.

Lastly, a study of coercive sexual behavior (sexual exploitation, rape, and sexual assault including forced drug searches) in British prisons (Banbury, 2004) found that victims were reluctant to report incidents because of fear (of repeat incidents, drug abstinence, disciplinary action, loss of parole), shame, staff reluctance to acknowledge existence of sexual relationships, and lack of confidential psychological/medical interventions for victims and perpetrators. The study, involving 408 adult male ex-prisoners, of whom approximately 80 percent were white, heterosexual, and under age thirty-three years, found that 1 percent had been sexually coerced into sexual intimacy and 4 percent had been subjected to forced drug searches. Victims were predominantly younger, passive, without group affiliations, homosexual, inexperienced, and drug dependent. Perpetrators were predominantly prisoners rather than staff, and approximately 50 percent of incidents involved more than one perpetrator—in half of these, multiple perpetrators (more than two) were present. The psychological problems following an incident of coercive same-sex sexual assault were also considerable for almost all victims—depression, shame, guilt, anxiety, nightmares, exacerbated drug use, suicide attempts, self-harm, anger, rage, and aggression.

The majority of incidents occurred in prison cells (usually involving cell mates), in the evening or during the night, especially following visits, and in the early stages of incarceration, when aggressive behavior, drug-related problems, and psychological and other effects of initial institutionalization may be more pronounced. Furthermore, Banbury's (2004) study revealed that victims of same-sex sexual coercion in prison may remain with the initial perpetrator or be pimped out, be intimidated not to report incidents, and suffer physical and psychological trauma, which increases their vulnerability.

Rotily, Galinier-Pujol, and Vernay-Vaisse (1995) assessed and compared the prevalence of same-sex sexual behavior among 295 male and 137 female injecting drug users and nonuser inmates, in two detention and short-stay prisons in southeastern France. The researchers found that the reported number of same-sex sexual activities (and partners) was two times higher among intravenous drug users (19 percent) compared to nonusers (9.5 percent).

An additional study of sexuality and same-sex sexual activities in a male prison in France was conducted by Merotte (2012). The main objectives of the study were to assess preconceived ideas on the part of the inmates about their sexuality, and the amount of shame and guilt they experienced surrounding those practices. Inmates from two prison facilities filled in (remand center for men in Loos-lez-Lille) and orally answered (detention center for men in Loos-lez-Lille) a ten-question questionnaire relating to different issues (i.e., changes in desire, changes in fantasies, masturbation habits, sexual intercourse, especially of a homosexual nature, sex in the visiting room, and finally other practices like voyeurism or exhibitionism) connected with their affective and sexual life. The findings of the study indicated that none of the inmates in the remand center and 7 percent of the prisoners in the detention center had had same-sex sexual relations in prison. Interestingly, all the inmates who had had same-sex sexual intercourse in prison stated that it was without their consent. Finally, homosexual intercourse—"the great taboo" (p. 122)—was perceived by all inmates as shameful and, consequently, inmates (consensually or coercively) engaging in homosexual acts were classified as "subhuman," dominated, and usable.

Barth (2012) conducted the first-ever study about the occurrence of same-sex sexual relations among male inmates in Germany and the associated effects of such behavior on inmates' gender roles and sexual practice. Analysis of thirty-five questionnaires revealed three major findings:

1. As regards to the possible effect of heterosexual sexual deprivation on the libido, a total of 45 percent of men reported losing their libido, 16 percent reported an increase, and 39 percent expressed no change at all.

2. No evidence was found in relation to possible tendency toward same-sex sexual activity by heterosexual inmates: the number of men who self-identified as homo- or bisexual was identical to the number of inmates who reported consensual same-sex sexual contacts while imprisoned. Moreover, only men who had had same-sex sexual relations prior to their imprisonment reported seeking inmates for inmate-to-inmate intimacy.

3. Some evidence was found of same-sex sexual violence: 20 percent of the inmates reported promises by prisoners to facilitate sexual contacts, 8.6 percent reported being blackmailed, 2.9 percent reported being threatened with physical violence, 22.9 percent stated that they were sexually harassed, and one participant (2.9 percent) reported being raped by an inmate.

In Hungary, Gyarmathy, Neaigus, and Szamado (2003) conducted a study on AIDS-related attitudes and the HIV risk behavior history of 551 male inmates (and 81 female inmates) in fourteen (out of the twenty-one) correctional facilities. Although the researchers clearly stated that they were unable to collect reliable information about what kind of sex inmates were having in prison, with whom, and to what extent they were using protection, informal conversations with the research participants led them to estimate that 9 percent of all participants had same-sex sexual relations in prison.

On the other side of the Mediterranean, in Africa, Niehaus (2002) analyzed the meanings of same-sex sexual relations in one South African male prison at Impalahoek. Based on interviews with eleven ex-prisoners, the researcher revealed that same-sex sexual relationships in prison express the hierarchical order of prison gangs and are sustained by violence and fear. According to his study, prisoners distinguish between consensual same-sex sexual relations and coercive male-male sexual relations. Consensual same-sex sexual relations follow a proposal and usually take place "within a framework of a formal relationships between a dominant lebosa ('the he one') and a subordinate picanini ('boy') or mfana wa misa ('boy wife')" (p. 91). The estimation of the frequency of such sexual relations varied from three men in a cell of twenty to two husbands and six wives in a cell of sixteen. Coercive same-sex sexual activity was found to be perpetrated by both prison officers and prison inmates and characterized by extreme pervasiveness. Furthermore, the majority of inmates' same-sex sexual rapes occurred between gang members (rapists) and newcomers (victims) as a form of initiation.

Gear (2005) thematically analyzed data based on in-depth interviews and focus group discussions with twenty-three male ex-prisoners and then-current prisoners in Gauteng Province, South Africa, to consider the moral economy established by a hegemonic inmate culture in which coerced same-sex sexual interactions are negotiated. Her study revealed that male prison populations tend to be divided into inmates identified as "men" and those identified as "women." "Women" are inmates who did not commit to proving their capacity for violence and, as such, are perceived as primarily the sexual property and servants of "men" and are often forcibly taken as "wives" (or "wyfies") by other prisoners in relationships known as "marriages." They are required, among other things, to be sexually available to their partners. "Men"/"husbands," on the other hand, provide materially for their "wives" through activity in the "business" of prison (i.e., provision of food, drugs, or protection). "Marriage"-type interactions are reportedly the most common form of sex in men's prisons and are accepted in the hegemonic inmate culture as the right place for sex to happen. In addition, Gear's study revealed that this prison moral economy as well as the gendered perception of these "women" (i.e., as being inferior and being to blame for what has happened to them) and the expectations of them (i.e., to passively accept that "men" will have same-sex sexual relations with them) have a negative influence on the victims' ability to report the abuse. In other words, coercive same-sex sexual activity is constructed as a gendering experience that changes men into "women," because "real men" do not allow themselves to be raped.

In his ethnographic study of the dynamics and prevalence of

HIV/AIDS in the Westville male prison in Durban, South Africa, Singh (2007) reported that sodomy, rape, sexual intercourse, and sexual assaults have been described as regular and normative occurrences in prison and, more generally, "an accepted normative practice in [all] South-African prisons" (p. 77). This awful reality is relevant to adult and youth prisoners as well as to awaiting-trial prisoners—regardless of their "innocent until proven guilty" status. Furthermore, Singh reveals that approximately 65 percent of the inmates in all South African prisons participate in consensual or coerced same-sex sexual relations in prison, regardless of the negative social stigma related to doing so. Finally, in a sole study conducted in Agodi Prison in Ibadan, Nigeria, regarding male inmates' knowledge about AIDS and sexual behavior, Okochi, Oladepo, and Ajuwon (1999–2000) revealed that 46.5 percent of the research participants (n = 177) engaged in risky (i.e., unprotected) same-sex sexual behaviors, and that young inmates had almost 2.5 times more same-sex sexual contacts than older inmates.

In the Middle East, Einat (2009) conducted a study of inmate sexual harassment and rape in seven maximum and medium security male prisons in Israel. The objectives of the study were threefold: (1) examination of inmates' views about same-sex sexual rape, (2) portrayal of prison slang used to describe same-sex sexual rape, rapists, and victims, and (3) analysis of the role of same-sex rape in the prisoners' social world. The study revealed that unlike many prison subcultures in other Western male prison facilities, where same-sex sexual rape is experienced as a practical way of obtaining a sense of dominance, Israeli inmates reject forced same-sex sexual behavior in prison and conceive same-sex sexual rapists and aggressors in prison as mentally and physically weak and, thus, contemptible. Consequently, the very few prisoners who sexually harassed or raped inmates in prison are socially isolated, negatively stigmatized, and given humiliating labels. Furthermore, two main explanations were given for the uniqueness of these findings and the fact that they stand in contrast to most other studies in this field: (1) the growing concern of Israeli inmates about HIV/AIDS over the last two decades leading to social marginalization of gay prisoners, classification of same-sex sexual rape in prison as misconduct, and abstention from engagement in coerced same-sex sexual activities in prison (see also Saum et al., 1995), and (2) the absolute objection to same-sex sexual rape by the three monotheistic religions—shared by approximately 97 percent of the prisoners (38.3 percent, Jews; 52.3 percent, Muslims; and 6.3 percent, Christians; Einat and Rabinovitz, forthcoming). As for the relevance of prison slang, Einat's (2009) study revealed that sexual terms once used to describe same-sex sexual rape and mock same-sex sexual rapists in prison are all caricatures of antisocial types applied to inmates who do not adhere to the unspoken code of prisoner behavior (for example, "punk" or "fag").

In an additional study, Einat (2013) interviewed a random sample of 151 adult inmates in two maximum security and two medium security male prisons in Israel in relation to the frequency of consensual same-sex sexual relations in prison. His study revealed that consensual same-sex sexual relations are very rare in Israeli prisons (i.e., only 2 percent of interviewees reported to have heard of a same-sex sexual act), and that such relationships are dishonorable and morally disgraceful.

In Pakistan, Altaf and colleagues (2009) assessed the sexual- and drug-related risk behaviors of male juvenile detainees. Information gathered from socio-demographic and sexual behavior questionnaires and from interviews with 321 juvenile detainees revealed that 7.8 percent (n = 25) of them have had same-sex sexual relations in prison, and eleven of them (3.4 percent of the total sample) stated that it was their first sexual engagement.

Lastly, in a novel, albeit nonacademic, article regarding Iranian prisons, Dehghan (2011) wrote that prison guards in several maximum security prisons in Iran provide condoms to criminal inmates, encouraging them to systematically rape political young opposition activists incarcerated with them. According to a series of smuggled letters written by prisoners and families of imprisoned activists, Iranian authorities are intentionally facilitating mass rape, using it as a form of punishment.

Conclusion

Consensual and coerced same-sex sexual activities among male inmates in prison are generally acknowledged by researchers and practitioners as an important matter. Although differing in their goals and data collection methods, researchers have found consensual or coerced same-sex sexual relations among male inmates to be central to daily prison life (Cotton and Groth, 1984; Fagan, Wennerstorm, and Miller, 1996; Kaminski, 2003).

The majority of Western and non-Western studies revealed that consensual and coerced same-sex sexual activities are firmly rooted in prison life (Ross and Richards, 2002; Toch, 1992). Most male inmates are deprived of heterosexual relationships and stripped of various traditional means of asserting their masculinity (Einat and Einat, 2000; Sykes, 1958; Toch, 1992). Yet these prisoners are subculturally expected to constantly demonstrate and illustrate their mental and physical power and dominance. All these elements together create extreme emotional, psychological, and perhaps physical distress (Tewksbury and West, 2000), which turns many, albeit not all, male inmates to intimidation and aggression, reestablishing their sense of dominance through same-sex sexual activities with consenting or coerced partners (Dumond, 2000; Hensley, 2002; Man and Cronan, 2002). Nevertheless, it should be pointed out that one study (Power et al., 1991), conducted in Scottish prisons, did not uncover a single case of sexual assault in male prisons, and additional research (Einat, 2009), conducted in several male Israeli prisons, revealed that such activities are very rare and rejected and that their perpetrators are conceived of by their peers as mentally and physically weak and, thus, contemptible.

Despite the frequency of coerced and consensual same-sex sexual relations in male prisons and their significance in the construction of prisons' subculture, research into male prison sexual relationships is currently insufficient and fails to adequately address central issues. Furthermore, most studies on the subject were conducted solely in US prisons. Hence, future research is needed to examine various aspects of such relationships, among them, (1) similarities and dissimilarities in meanings, functions, and implications of same-sex sexual relationships in different cultures, (2) relationships between religion and engagement in same-sex sexual activities, (3) correlations between participation in same-sex sexual relationships and observance of religion, and (4) connections between involvement in same-sex sexual relationships in prison and types of offenses. The challenge for researchers is, therefore, to find ways to produce valid, reliable, and comparative research concerning same-sex sexual relationships in male prisons and to increase our understanding of the nature, implications, and consequences of such relationships in male prison subculture.

Lastly, greater knowledge and awareness of this issue can help reduce sexual violence behind prison walls (Hensley, 2000a; Struckman-Johnson et al., 1996) and the related health problems, which have severe implications for prisoners, institutional staff, and the general public, alike.

9

Local Perspectives

Danielle McDonald and Alexis Miller

The United States incarcerates more of its citizens than any other industrialized nation. Currently, 2.2 million US citizens are imprisoned in jails, state prisons, or the federal prison system within this country (Mauer, 2013). Over the last thirty years, the prison and jail populations have increased a staggering 500 percent, which has led to overcrowding within the system causing an increase in violence and overwhelming staff (Mauer, 2013). In 2011, for example, the overcrowding within California's prison system drew national attention after multiple riots occurred. The California prison system had been designed to house 80,000 inmates, but 140,000 inmates were imprisoned within the system (Gottesdiener, 2011). Sexual violence within the prison system also began to garner national attention as reports of sexual assault began to surface in male and female institutions in the late 1990s and early 2000s. The institution has the responsibility of ensuring that all inmates are housed safely and securely. Physical and sexual violence within correctional facilities violates an inmate's Eighth Amendment right against cruel and unusual punishment. However, when an institution becomes severely overcrowded, staff have more difficulty ensuring the safety of the inmates.

The issues of overcrowding and sexual violence were eventually addressed by the federal government. In 2011, the US Supreme Court upheld a lower court's ruling that the State of California would be required to reduce that state's prison population to 137 percent capacity within two years due to the overcrowded prison conditions (Carson and Sabol, 2012). The federal government also intervened in the case of sexual assault creating the Prison Rape Elimination Act (PREA) of 2003, which has a zero-tolerance policy for sexual assault within any correctional facility (PREA, 2003).

In this chapter, we examine published newspaper articles from across the United States on the topic of sexual assault and female inmates three years prior to the passage of PREA and five years after it was implemented to better understand changes in female inmate sexual assault since the passage of PREA. This project began in the fall of 2008 after we read newspaper accounts of the sexual assaults of multiple female inmates in a privately run prison in Kentucky called Otter Creek. The sexual assaults occurred over a period of three years with an eventual twenty-three charges. The number of sexual assaults and the length of time over which they occurred were alarming because PREA had been signed into law in the fall of 2003. PREA has a specific zero-tolerance clause stating that sexual assault will not be tolerated at any correctional facility. However, multiple cases of sexual assault with multiple victims and offenders were documented at Otter Creek several years later. As we found out, Otter Creek turned out to have many problems.

Otter Creek Correctional Center

Located in eastern Kentucky, Otter Creek Correctional Center is a privately owned and operated prison, managed by Corrections Corporation of America (CCA), which is based in Nashville, Tennessee. Originally designed as a minimum security prison located in Wheelwright, Kentucky, Otter Creek, with 656 beds, was reclassified as a medium security facility in 2000 (Brady, 2009). After issues with housing Indiana inmates, including a riot, the facility was closed for a short time in 2005. It reopened on July 12, 2005, with a new contract to house 400 women from Kentucky's prison system. In September of 2005, Otter Creek agreed to house additional inmates, thus eighty Hawaiian inmates were shipped from Brush, Colorado, to Otter Creek. The Hawaiian inmates were transferred from the private prison in Colorado to Kentucky due to sexual assault allegations between staff and inmates in Colorado (Mitchell, 2005). By October of 2007, 400 Kentucky inmates and 175 inmates from the Hawaiian correctional system were housed in the Otter Creek Correctional Complex.

In 2008, several news agencies in Kentucky started releasing information concerning allegations of sexual assault on female inmates in Otter Creek. However prior to the 2008 reports of sexual assault, Otter Creek had experienced a series of other problems reported in the news (Brady, 2009). For instance, the Kentucky State Police reported in 2006 that a guard was arrested and charged with sexual abuse of an inmate. Following that arrest, a drug counselor from the facility was arrested and charged with drug trafficking, and by the end of 2007 at least three Hawaiian inmates were reported dead at Otter Creek. The deceased inmates' families all stated the deaths were due to inadequate medical care and deliberate indifference to the inmates' health problems. Finally in 2008, before the alleged rape reports surfaced, the warden's secretary smuggled a loaded .22-caliber gun into the prison and committed suicide in the warden's office (Brady, 2009).

Nine months later in October of 2008, the initial reports of rape started to arrive. The first allegations came from a letter written by a Hawaiian inmate housed at Otter Creek. The letter was initially sent to her mother, and the mother forwarded it on to a Hawaiian newspaper (Brady, 2009). The letter and report stated a corrections officer entered the inmate's cell in the early morning hours of October 16, 2007, and "demanded that she perform sex acts" (Brady, 2009, p. 7). The accused corrections officer was fired, but the reports of sexual assault in the prison continued. Investigators from Hawaii found "that five corrections officials, including a chaplain, had been charged with having sex with inmates" over the three years the Hawaiian inmates had been housed in Otter Creek (Brady, 2009, p. 7). Of these cases, four of the accused were convicted, and three more cases involving corrections officers were turned over to law enforcement. By 2009, the *New York Times* reported Kentucky was investigating twenty-three acts of sexual assault, all at Otter Creek, dating back to 2006.

By July/August of 2009, investigative reports on the Otter Creek Correctional Complex conducted by the Commonwealth's Department of Corrections and Hawaii's Department of Public Safety exposed significant staff shortages, low wages, and poor employee morale (Brady, 2009; Urbina, 2009). As reported by state monitors in

Kentucky, the sexual assaults stemmed partly from the fact that 81 percent of the employees at Otter Creek were men (with only 19 percent female staff) (Urbina, 2009). Instead of ending the contract with CCA, Kentucky agreed to extend the contract with CCA and Otter Creek for one year, in exchange for an agreement that CCA would aggressively seek more female corrections employees at Otter Creek, even offering a sign-on bonus for those women hired (Brady, 2009).

By January 2010, the Hawaiian inmates had been moved back to Hawaii, and it became clear CCA was not going to be able to fulfill the demand to increase the number of female corrections employees at Otter Creek. However, instead of shutting the facility down completely, Governor Steve Beshear announced that he would move the 400 women housed at Otter Creek to a public institution in western Kentucky, and 700 male inmates from the western Kentucky facility would be moved to the privately operated Otter Creek facility. Many critics cited this exchange of inmates as a reward for CCA because instead of being fined for the continual violations of the contract and inmates' rights, they were rewarded with 700 inmates. Otter Creek was now above their "bed capacity," which they had not filled since the removal of the Hawaiian inmates in August of 2009. Finally, in April 2012, officials announced that the State of Kentucky would *not* renew the contract with CCA's Otter Creek facility, thus leaving it to shut its doors by the end of June (Burks, 2012).

Otter Creek is no longer open, but the problems it presented were never truly addressed. We began to question if this type of behavior was occurring at other correctional facilities that held female inmates or if Otter Creek was an isolated incident. Was not PREA supposed to stop this type of criminal behavior, and if not stop it completely, address it as soon as it was discovered?

PREA and Female Inmates

Several human rights organizations as early as 1996 were compiling reports on custodial rape in women's prisons (Amnesty International, 1999; Human Rights Watch, 1996). In response to these reports, legislation was introduced to Congress addressing female sexual abuse (or rape) in prison. As a part of the original Violence Against Women Act of 1994, the Custodial Sexual Abuse Act was introduced. This piece of legislation specifically addressed female inmate victims of staff-initiated sexual misconduct. The legislation was unsuccessful in getting the support it needed to be a part of the Violence Against Women Act of 1998. In fact, according to Smith (2008), it "failed to garner enough support even for consideration" (p. 10) and was never reintroduced.

Five years later, after estimating that nearly one million prisoners had been sexually assaulted while in government custody, Congress unanimously passed PREA (PREA, 2003). This act was signed into law by then-president George W. Bush on September 4, 2003. Along with the goal of ending all sexual violence in corrections, PREA (1) established zero-tolerance standards toward rape in correctional facilities perpetrated by inmates or staff, (2) directed the Bureau of Justice Statistics to carry out a comprehensive annual statistical review and analysis of incidences and effects of prison rape, (3) directed the Department of Justice to establish a review panel that would hold public hearings on prison rape addressing the three facilities with the highest incidents of prison rape and the two with the lowest, (4) charged the National Institute of Corrections to provide training and assistance to the field of corrections in reducing or ending all prison rape, and (5) directed the attorney general to develop grants for the states to safeguard their budgets (PREA, 2003).

Smith (2008) asked the question, What happened over the course of those five years that brought Congress from *refusing to consider* a bill aimed at eliminating prison sexual violence to *unanimously passing* PREA? She surmised that some of the changes were due to the increase of white males in the prison system and concerns of government liability for prison rape. More importantly the more apparent reason for the change was the ever-growing fear by society of male-on-male–perpetrated prison rape, thus *homosexual rape*. Smith (2008) states that "society takes it as a given that women will be victimized both in the free world and in custody," but "the image of male rape was much more disturbing to members of Congress" (p. 10). To illustrate this issue, one only has to look at the original version of PREA, which did *not* include instances of sexual violence against women in custody. Essentially women were an addition to the second version of PREA with the inclusion of sexual violence perpetrated by correctional officers or staff, which is more often the case with incarcerated women (Smith, 2008).

Even with the inclusion of women in the final version of the act, critics still contend that PREA has a larger focus on male rape victimization in prison, specifically on white male inmate victims. Regardless of Congress or society's attentiveness to male victims of rape in prison, women are the fastest-growing population under correctional supervision and are more likely to be raped by a staff member while in jail custody (Beck, Harrison, and Adams, 2007).

This occurrence of sexual violation led us to question how much of an impact PREA was having on female inmates. Since we were able to gather so much information from the newspaper on Otter Creek, we decided that newspaper articles published from across the United States prior to PREA and after would be used to examine if any changes had taken place in the sexual assault of female inmates since the passage of PREA. Specifically the following research questions were addressed: (1) Who is involved in the sexual assault of female inmates, and where are these crimes taking place? (2) How are offenders being punished? and (3) How was the offense portrayed in the newspaper article by the offender, victim, and the media?

Methods

Content analysis was utilized to examine newspaper articles printed on the topic of female inmates and sexual assault in the United States. This process allowed for comparisons to be made between material before PREA was implemented and material published afterward. This method was chosen because it allowed the researchers to examine a body of text and pull out themes by counting and recording the number of times the incident occurred (Neuman, 1997).

First, variables were constructed and defined. The following variables were created to better understand who was involved in the criminal act and where it took place, including sex of the offender (male/female), offender's position at work (corrections officer, medical staff, educational staff, religious staff, law enforcement, bailiff, transportation staff, kitchen/laundry staff, and warden), the location of the crime (state prison, private prison, federal prison, jail, community corrections, during transport, courthouse, private jail, private prison, private community corrections, home detention), and where the inmate was incarcerated at the time of the offense (state prison,

jail, federal prison, private prison, community corrections, home detention, private prison, private jail, private community corrections).
The variable of offender's charge was used to examine the crimes offenders were charged with, while the variables of offender's conviction, offender's sentence, and offender's work status after the offense
were used to examine how perpetrators were being punished for their
crimes. How the offender, victim, and media perceived the crime also
was examined by looking at statements made by the victim and offender as well as titles and themes of newspaper articles. Their perceptions were categorized as sexual misconduct/institutional sex, consensual sex, rape/sexual assault, and bribery for goods or protection.

Second, a sampling parameter was defined and a sample of articles was collected using LexisNexis Academic's database of US
newspaper articles and wires. The search was confined to newspaper
articles printed three years prior to the implementation of PREA (August 1, 2000, to August 31, 2003) and five years after (September 1,
2003, to August 31, 2008) using the search words *female inmate* and
sexual assault. The time period of three years prior to the passage of
the act was selected in order to gain a better understanding of what
was happening immediately before the act was created, while the period of five years after the act was selected to give the act enough
time to be implemented. This search resulted in a return of 984 newspaper articles from across the United States. Articles that did not
focus on adult female inmates as victims of sexual assault were removed from the sample along with articles that were identical repli-
cas and those that discussed the problem in general terms but did not
focus on any specific case. The total number of articles examined
was 496 with 115 of these articles published prior to PREA and 381
printed after the act was implemented.

Next, a code sheet was created to assist with content analysis.
Both manifest coding and latent coding were used when recording
the data. Manifest coding was used to determine how often something occurred and required the researcher to simply record the information onto the code sheet. The following variables were entered
using manifest coding: the sex of the offender, the offender's position, what the offender was charged and convicted of, the offender's
sentence, the location of the crime, the location of the inmate serving
time, and the offender's work status. Latent coding where the researcher "looks for the underlying, implicit meaning in the context of

a text" was used to examine the variables of how the offense was portrayed by the offender, the victim, and the media (Neuman, 1997, p. 276). Intercoder reliability, used to improve the reliability of the content analysis, relies on both researchers to code the data individually and then compare their results for consistency (Neuman, 1997).

Finally, the data was taken from the code sheets and entered into a Statistical Product and Service Solutions (SPSS) database, where the data could be further analyzed. Cross tabulations were used to examine the frequency of the variables prior to the implementation of PREA and afterwards.

Results

Who is involved in the sexual assault of female inmates, and where are these crimes taking place? The overwhelming majority of the offenders, both prior to and after the implementation of PREA, were male. Prior to PREA, only two of the total 110 offenders were female and after the act was implemented only one of the total 182 offenders was female. The majority of offenders (75 percent) held the position of corrections officer both before and after PREA. The top four positions held by offenders prior to the act were corrections officer (75 percent), law enforcement (8 percent), kitchen/laundry staff (3 percent), and medical staff (3 percent). The top four positions held by offenders after the act were corrections officer (75 percent), law enforcement (9 percent), bailiff (2 percent), and jail/prison administrator (2 percent).

Most victims were being held in a jail with the next most common place of incarceration being state prison. Prior to PREA the top three places inmate victims were being incarcerated included jail (65 percent), state prison (27 percent), and federal prison (1 percent). After PREA, the top four places inmate victims were being incarcerated included jail (74 percent), state prison (13 percent), federal prison (4 percent), and private prison (3 percent). Therefore, after the implementation of PREA, the number of published reports of female inmates being sexually assaulted in state prisons decreased, while the number of incidents in jails increased.

The offense most commonly occurred within a jail both prior to and after PREA; however, the number of incidents occurring within state prisons decreased after PREA. Prior to the act, the top four lo-cations for the crime were in jail (62 percent), in state prison (26 per-cent), during transport (3 percent), and in federal prison (1 percent). After the act was implemented, the top five locations where the crime occurred were in jail (65 percent), in state prison (12 percent), during transport (7 percent), in federal prison (4 percent), and in private prisons (3 percent).

How are offenders being punished? Prior to PREA and after, most offenders were fired or resigned from their jobs. Some slight differences could be found in offenders' work status before and after the act. Prior to PREA, offenders were fired (40 percent), resigned (25 percent), suspended without pay (18 percent), placed on paid ad-ministrative leave (11 percent), jailed (5 percent), or placed on un-paid administrative leave (5 percent). After PREA, offenders were fired (40 percent), resigned (21 percent), placed on paid administra-tive leave (15 percent), jailed (10 percent), suspended without pay (6 percent), or placed in unpaid administrative leave (5 percent).

Prior to PREA and after, most offenders were charged with the crime of sexual misconduct or sexual assault/rape. Prior to the act, most offenders were charged with sexual misconduct (49 percent), sexual assault/rape (14 percent), sodomy (7 percent), and second-degree sexual assault (3 percent). After PREA, most offenders were charged with sexual misconduct (52 percent), sexual assault/rape (14 percent), second-degree sexual assault (6 percent), and sodomy (2 percent). The results for the crime the offender was convicted of were similar to the crimes the offender was charged with, with the two most common crimes, both before and after PREA, being sexual miscon-duct (30 percent pre-PREA and 23 percent post-PREA) and sexual as-sault/rape (20 percent pre-PREA and 18 percent post-PREA).

Some changes have occurred since the implementation of PREA in the type of sentence one is most likely to receive. Prior to the act, the most common sentence was probation (28 percent) followed by jail (22 percent) and prison (8 percent). After the implementation of the act, the most common sentence was jail (34 percent), probation (26 percent), and prison (16 percent). Therefore, after the implemen-tation of PREA, the number of published reports of offenders being sentenced to jail or state prisons has increased.

How was the offense portrayed in the newspaper article by the offender, the victim, and the media? Some changes came about in how offenders portrayed their offense in the media before and after the act. Prior to the act, offenders were more likely to state the sexual act was consensual (61 percent), they were not guilty (25 percent), or they participated as part of a bribe (11 percent). After the act was implemented, offenders were more likely to state they were not guilty (45 percent), the act was consensual (43 percent), or they participated in a bribe (2 percent). However, little changed in how victims portrayed themselves in the media. Most victims stated they had been raped/sexually assaulted (55 percent pre-PREA and 54 percent post-PREA) or were bribed (30 percent both pre- and post-PREA).

Prior to PREA, the media tended to portray the offense as sexual misconduct (38 percent), rape/sexual assault (36 percent), bribery (13 percent), or consensual (10 percent). After PREA, the media was much less likely to portray the offense as a bribe (1 percent) or consensual (1 percent) and were more likely to report it was sexual misconduct (54 percent) or rape/sexual assault (42 percent).

Discussion

In the current study, both prior to PREA and after, the typical offender was a male correctional officer and the offense most commonly occurred within a jail. Similar results were found in the Bureau of Justice Statistics' national survey of administrative records, where incidents of sexual assault for both male and female inmates reported to correctional officers in jails and prisons were examined. Beck, Harrison and Adams (2007) concluded that 80 percent of victims of substantiated sexual assault in jail were female, 79 percent of the perpetrators of these crimes were male, and 98 percent of the time they held the professional position of correctional officer.

State prisons showed a decrease in the number of published sexual assaults against female inmates after the implementation of PREA. Prior to the act, for example, 26 percent of the published sexual assaults of female inmates occurred within state prisons, while after the act this number was reduced to 12 percent. Knowing how much of an impact PREA had on this decline and what other factors may have influenced this result is difficult. One explanation, for example, could be that females are not as likely to be assaulted by staff in prison as males. Beck, Harrison, and Adams (2007) found the majority of victims of substantiated sexual assault by a staff person in state and federal prisons were male (65 percent), and the offender in 58 percent of these cases was a female. However, one cannot discount that female inmates make up a total of 6.8 percent of the state and federal prison population, but are still 35 percent of the victims of substantiated sexual assaults perpetrated by staff (Guerino, Harrison, and Sabol, 2011).

The current study concluded most offenders, both before and after PREA, were charged and convicted of sexual misconduct or sexual assault/rape. Since the implementation of PREA, offenders also were more likely to be sentenced to jail or prison, while prior to PREA, probation was the most common sentence. Most offenders also were fired or resigned after the offense was reported. This is similar to what Beck, Harrison, and Adams (2007) found, where offenders at prisons and jails were fired or resigned in 77 percent of substantiated cases against male and female inmates. Beck, Harrison, and Adams (2007) also found 56 percent of staff involved in substantiated sexual misconduct cases against male and female inmates were arrested or referred for prosecution, with 24 percent of offenders being arrested and 45 percent of offenders being referred for prosecution. Knowing the percentages of all offenders who were arrested or referred for prosecution is difficult in the current study because not all published incidents had later articles that provided updates on the case.

The current study found offenders were more likely to state they were not guilty (45 percent) and less likely to state the act was consensual (43 percent) after the implementation of PREA. Increased recognition and prosecution of staff in inmate sexual misconduct cases since the passage of PREA may be why more offenders portray themselves as not guilty in the media. However, the number of offenders who view the offense as consensual is alarming. Sexual contact in an institution between staff and an inmate can never be consensual due to the power differentiation between an inmate and a staff person. Even though PREA has a zero-tolerance policy for such behavior, correctional staff do not always seem to view the behavior as nonconsensual. Beck, Harrison, and Adams (2007), for example, found 57 percent of substantiated sexual misconduct cases between an inmate and a staff person were recorded by staff as being a "willing relationship" (p. 6).

After PREA, the media was much less likely to portray the offense as a bribe (1 percent) or consensual (1 percent) and were more likely to report it was sexual misconduct (54 percent) or rape/sexual assault (42 percent). This change in how the media portrays sexual assault in prisons and jails can have a big impact on the public and how they view these cases. Prisons and jails are not typically open to the public. Much of what the public knows about prisons and jails is learned from television shows, movies, and news reports. Levan, Polzer, and Downing (2011) found, in their study of movie portrayals of male-on-male inmate sexual assault, mixed messages of myths and truths within the films making it difficult for the consumer to tell the difference. Levan, Polzer, and Downing stated, "For issues concerning sexual violence among inmates, these depictions may have varying results, depending on the type of portrayal. If victims of sexual abuse are characters, which we, as audience members, are meant to be sympathetic toward, then these depictions may increase the attention and empathy given to the victims" (p. 675). Perhaps if the media continues to portray sexual offenses in female institutions as sexual assault or sexual misconduct, the public may be more likely to empathize with the victims of these crimes and demand changes occur within these institutions.

Conclusion

The current study found the majority of published cases in the newspaper on the topic of female inmate victims of sexual assault occurred within jails. This finding was corroborated by the Bureau of Justice Statistics' study, which examined administrative records in adult correctional facilities (Beck, Harrison, and Adams, 2007). This finding suggests increased attention needs to be given to jails on this topic.

The Bureau of Justice Statistics has been keeping track of the occurrences of sexual assault in prisons and jails by having a sample of inmates complete the self-report National Inmate Survey on their own sexual victimization within the last twelve months. The 2007 report on jail inmates found that 3.2 percent of all jail inmates, both male and female, reported they experienced sexual violence. In about half of these incidents another inmate was the offender with the other half of offenders being staff (Beck and Harrison, 2008). These numbers seem low, but fear of reporting the incident may keep this statistic below what we would expect. Human Rights Watch (1996) concluded female victims of sexual assault by staff in prison rarely report the abuse due to a fear of retaliation by the correctional officers. One may not be willing to risk overcoming this fear to make a report, especially if the victim believes that her claim of victimization may not be substantiated after an investigation. In 2006, for example, only 18 percent of all staff sexual misconduct complaints were substantiated; most were not substantiated due to a lack of evidence (Beck, Harrison, and Adams, 2007). Fear and shame also likely play a part in victims' unwillingness to make a report. According to Beck (2012), 79 percent of male and female inmates who experienced staff sexual misconduct stated they felt shame and 72 percent stated they felt guilt as a result of their victimization. Therefore, even though the results of the survey are anonymous, those who complete the survey may still feel afraid or too ashamed to admit what happened to them.

More recent attempts have been made to alleviate a respondent's fear of retaliation for completing a survey on sexual assault in correctional facilities. The National Former Prisoner Survey was developed to be distributed to a sample of parolees who are asked about their experiences during their time in jail, prison, or community correctional facility. This survey is completed when the respondent is under community supervision and no longer incarcerated. The National Former Prisoner Survey found 9.6 percent of former state inmates, both male and female, had experienced sexual assault during their incarceration with most of these incidents (7.5 percent) occurring within a state prison and 1.8 percent in a jail (Beck, 2012). The number of reported sexual assaults in prison on the National Former Prisoner Survey is much higher than the 4.8 percent reported by inmates in 2008 on the National Inmate Survey. However, the same is not true for jail inmates. The National Inmate Survey found 3.2 percent of all jail inmates had experienced sexual violence while incarcerated in a jail, but the National Former Prisoner Survey only found 1.8 percent of former state prisoners experienced sexual victimization while in jail (Beck and Harrison, 2008). Therefore, this newer survey may not be capturing all of the incidents of sexual victimization within jails either, further supporting the need to create a survey that focuses specifically on the jailed population.

The current study also concluded offenders still portrayed themselves in the media as engaging in consensual sex with female inmates 43 percent of the time. This finding was corroborated by Beck, Harrison, and Adams (2007), when they found 57 percent of substantiated cases of sexual misconduct between an inmate and staff were documented by staff as being willing even though PREA has a zero-tolerance policy for such behavior. How staff view sexual assault and sexual contact between staff and inmates is directly related to how wardens implement PREA within their facilities. Each warden has the ability to implement the policy within his or her individual institution in order to avoid a one-size-fits-all approach (Obama, 2012). However, this flexibility could be problematic as found in the study by Moster and Jeglic (2009), who surveyed state prison wardens on the topic of male-on-male inmate sexual assault post-PREA. Only 49 percent of the state prison wardens surveyed stated they had enforced the policy of zero tolerance (Moster and Jeglic, 2009). The successful implementation of this act will depend a great deal on the leadership of the wardens at these institutions and their buy-in as stakeholders. As President Barack Obama stated when addressing the nation on the topic of PREA, "in addition to adopting such standards, the success of PREA in combating sexual abuse in confinement facilities will depend on effective agency and facility leadership and the development of an agency culture that prioritizes efforts to combat sexual abuse" (Obama, 2012, p. 1).

This research project was inspired by the newspaper articles published about the sexual assaults that occurred at CCA's private prison Otter Creek in Kentucky. The analysis of the sample of newspaper articles selected for this project did not find sexual assaults to be occurring as often at private facilities as it did within state and local facilities. Otter Creek was shut down in June of 2012 after the State of Kentucky did not renew its contract with the privately run prison (Burks, 2012). However, the reliance of states on private prisons will continue to be hotly debated. In Ohio, for example, the governor proposed in his 2012 state budget that five state-run prisons be sold to private companies to help reduce the cost of operating the prisons for the state. After the governor's announcement, concerns were raised regarding the impact of this transfer on jobs as well as conflicts of interest within the governor's staff (Guillen, 2011).

10

Further Implications

Tammy L. Castle and Catherine D. Marcum

One of the main punishment philosophies implemented by our corrections system, whether on the prison or jail level, is incapacitation. Incapacitation refers to the incarceration of individuals in a correctional facility, with the intention of restricting movement and depriving inmates of the freedoms and liberties they otherwise would have enjoyed had they not been incarcerated. In addition, incapacitation serves to protect the community from additional harms by removing the offender from society. However, since the offender then becomes a captive of the federal or state correctional system, the correctional system has the responsibility of keeping the inmates safe during their period of incarceration. Furthermore, correctional administrators must consider the safety of staff working in these facilities. Prisons and jails are infamous for the victimization of their residents, whether via physical and sexual assault, theft, or property damage (Wolff and Shi, 2009). As a result, inmates are constantly on guard to protect themselves from potential victimization; thus, they tend to be extremely untrusting of fellow inmates (Bowker, 1980; Irwin, 1980; Toch, 1977).

Thanks in part to films and television shows featuring prisons, a stereotypical assumption has arisen that entrance into an incarcerating facility as a resident (aka inmate) equates to guaranteed experience with sexual victimization. While the fear of sexual victimization upon incarceration is more prevalent among inmates than the reality

(Tewksbury, 1989a), sexual victimization does occur and remains a problem for our correctional systems. Correctional administrators are forced to deal with both the health concerns of victimization, such as the spread of disease, as well as the violence associated with it.

Reported rates of sexual assault inside correctional facilities have varied from 1 percent to 41 percent (Wolff and Shi, 2008), generally due to two factors: (1) the underreporting of occurrences, which is attributed to stigma of the assault and fear of retribution (Struckman-Johnson et al., 1996), and (2) methodological variation in regard to the conceptualization and operationalization of sexual assault (Beck and Harrison, 2007a; Struckman-Johnson and Struckman-Johnson, 2006; Wolff and Shi, 2009). Due to the discrepancy in rates of sexual victimization among these studies, Gaes and Goldberg (2004) performed a meta-analysis and estimated that the most likely average rate of sexual assault is 1.9 percent, even though some correctional institutions report much higher rates.

The most extensive study to date on the prevalence of sexual victimization in prison was conducted by the US Department of Justice as part of the Prison Rape Elimination Act (PREA) of 2003 annual data collection activities. The National Former Prisoner Survey provided data from 18,256 interviews with former state inmates under parole supervision. The parole offices from which the researchers drew their sample were selected randomly, and only former inmates were used in an effort to increase the reporting of incidents that currently incarcerated inmates may fear reporting due to retaliation. The final report was published in May 2012 and respondents were interviewed about any incidents that occurred during any period of incarceration in any and all types of facilities (jails, prison, or community) (Bureau of Justice Statistics, 2012a).

Some of the more startling figures included the following: 9.6 percent of former state inmates reported one or more incidents of sexual victimization during the last period of incarceration (in jails, prisons, and postrelease facilities), with the highest percentage (7.5 percent) of those incidents occurring in state prisons. In the state prisons, sexual victimization by other inmates was three times higher for females (13.7 percent) than males (4.2 percent). Moreover, 1.2 percent of all inmates reported they unwillingly had sex or sexual contact with facility staff, and rates of victimization were higher for males who identified as homosexual or gay (39 percent) as opposed to those who identified as heterosexual (3.5 percent) (Bureau of Justice Statistics, 2012a).

In addition to sexual assault and rape, which is illegal both in and out of prison, inmates do engage in consensual sexual activity. As Sykes (1958) outlined in *The Society of Captives: A Study of Maximum Security Prison,* the deprivation of heterosexual relationships represents one of the "pains of imprisonment" that result in frustration and can exacerbate psychological issues, because "a society composed exclusively of men tends to generate anxieties in its members concerning their masculinity regardless of whether or not they are coerced, bribed, or seduced into an overt homosexual liaison" (p. 67). The pains of imprisonment, however, are not exclusive to men; women also experience the deprivation of intimacy. Consensual sexual activity still occurs among inmates and between inmates and staff in secret because it is forbidden in correctional facilities. For that reason, academics and practitioners are forced to consider the multiple layers of the decidedly controversial issue that is sexual behavior in prison, which includes health concerns, safety issues, and the psychological impact of the deprivation applicable to both sexes. The purpose of this text was to present updated research on a variety of issues regarding sexual activity in prison, whether these concerns involve the participants, corrections systems, or legislative bodies attempting to combat and punish this behavior. Experts in the field have discussed a wide range of topics that have provided the reader with a full grasp of the issue of sexual behavior in prison.

Health Concerns

As cited previously, of the pains of imprisonment—which include loss of liberty, goods and services, autonomy, and security—Sykes (1958) identified the lack of heterosexual relationships as one of the most psychologically damaging. According to his deprivation model, the frustrations from the pains of imprisonment influence an inmate's behavior in a variety of ways once incarcerated. More specifically, he argued that inmate misconduct was a direct result of experiencing these pains.

For the inmate, moving from uninhibited freedoms in the "outside" world to constant regulation and supervision in a locked institution can be extremely frustrating. Individuals who are incarcerated have limited, if any, autonomy and are generally not permitted to engage in any kind of intimate relationships inside the facility. During visits with intimate partners from outside the facility, physical contact is usually forbidden, including hand holding, hugging, and kissing.

The shock of incarceration and the deprivation of intimacy may cause inmates to act out in ways seeking to satisfy these desires, such as the participation in homosexual activity that they would not otherwise engage in if not incarcerated. In other words, inmates who identify as heterosexual on the "outside" may choose to engage in homosexual relationships while incarcerated in order to fulfill the desire for intimacy and sexual relations. A consequence of unprotected homosexual activity in correctional facilities is the increased risk of infection with multiple sexually transmitted diseases, including HIV/AIDS.

As Potter and Rosky noted in the chapter on health issues in prison, the transmission of STDs is a major health concern for inmates as the infection rates tend to be higher than in the general population. Moreover, because most inmates are eventually released back into society, the spread of disease also represents a public health concern. For this reason, the Centers for Disease Control and Prevention (2001) have recommended routine screening for HIV/AIDS in correctional facilities in addition to prevention counseling. Of the correctional facilities offering this type of counseling, prevention efforts have generally centered on educational programs for inmates and staff. In these programs, the emphasis is placed on the dangers and health risks of unprotected sex and how to use barrier methods to prevent transmission to one's partner. Further, information is usually provided on the outlets available for reporting inappropriate behavior within the prison facility. However, while preventative education is important, it is not a panacea, and other methods must be explored for preventing the spread of disease.

One such prevention method involves the distribution of condoms to inmates. Although a controversial proposal in the United States, this practice is more common in other parts of the world. Some of the largest penal systems in countries such as Brazil and South Africa, as well as smaller penal systems in Australia and Canada, distribute condoms to inmates specifically to combat the spread of disease (Stöver et al., 2001). In fact, some countries have faced civil liability suits for not distributing condoms in their prisons.

For example, prior to the introduction of condoms in 1996, a South African prisoner who had contracted HIV sued the Department of Correctional Services for not providing education on the risks of STDs as well as for not providing condoms to inmates. The case was settled out of court but set the precedent for a similar lawsuit in New South Wales, Australia. In that case, fifty-two inmates sued the Department of Corrective Services for not providing condoms. Before the lawsuit could be settled, the correctional administrators initiated a pilot program in three of the country's prisons to test condom distribution. Based on its success, the program was implemented in all New South Wales institutions and even dental dams were provided to female inmates (Yap et al., 2007).

Like South Africa, the United States also has one of the largest penal systems in the world. However, few correctional facilities in the United States allow jail and prison administrators to legally distribute condoms, although access to condoms is more commonly found in jails. In the Los Angeles and San Francisco city jails, administrators allow a variety of community organizations to distribute condoms. Similarly, in the metropolitan jails of other big cities (such as Rikers Island in New York City and jails in Philadelphia and Washington, DC) correctional administrators may provide free condoms on a limited basis or make them available for purchase by inmates through the commissary.

In prisons, on the other hand, only two states currently distribute condoms. Inmates in Vermont may receive condoms from community organizations, such as Vermont CARES, or condoms are available via the prison health center. The State of Mississippi also distributes condoms. However, the practice is limited to married inmates participating in a conjugal visitation program, and even then distribution is restricted to two condoms per visit (Harm Reduction in Prison Coalition, 2011). Condoms are not offered in the other four states (California, New York, New Mexico, and Washington) that allow conjugal visitation.

The resistance by correctional administrators to sponsoring condom distribution programs in US prisons is primarily due to the fact that condoms are considered contraband. Sexual activity, sometimes including masturbation, is prohibited among inmates, defined as an administrative infraction, and punished accordingly. Correctional administrators argue that distributing condoms would be the equivalent of condoning illegal behavior in the facility. Furthermore, the correctional staff identify condoms as a potential safety risk given that they could be utilized by inmates for other illegal purposes.

Despite the assumed negatives of condom distribution, empirical evidence has indicated that condoms do significantly decrease the spread of HIV/AIDS and other STDs (National Institute of Allergy and Infectious Diseases, 2001; Warner et al., 2006). Furthermore, studies performed in prisons have found positive outcomes regarding condom distribution. The feasibility of condom distribution has been supported, as it is not obtrusive to prison routine and distribution programs can be easily replicated to other facilities (Dolan, Lowe, and Shearer, 2004; May and Williams, 2002; Yap et al., 2007). Studies in Australia and the United States have shown that condom distribution in prisons is supported by inmates and correctional staff, especially after the success of the program has been demonstrated in other facilities.

As mentioned previously, an assumption can be found among correctional staff that condoms present a hazard and the distribution of them in prison could create safety risks. However, the empirical research to date does not support this assumption. May and Williams's (2002) study on condom access in the United States found that condoms alone did not constitute a threat to security. Furthermore, in Australia, Dolan, Lowe, and Shearer (2004) and Yap and colleagues (2007) found that the only substantiated cases of misuse of the condoms was for water balloon fights and littering. As Potter and Rosky argued, the fears regarding filling condoms with sand and using them as weapons have not materialized.

Correctional staff also reported concerns over the utilization of condoms to conceal contraband, such as drugs. In Yap and colleagues' (2007) study 29 percent of inmates surveyed indicated that they did know inmates who used condoms as storage balloons for drugs. However, the authors found no increase in drug use as a result of the condom implementation programs; thus, using the condoms for drug storage was simply a matter of convenience and not due to the introduction of condoms into the facility. In other words, inmates will use whatever is available to store contraband. On the other hand, Dolan, Lowe, and Shearer (2004) found no recorded drug concealment in facilities that distributed condoms. Lastly, and possibly the most important finding, no prisons have reversed their prison distribution policy once it was initiated, which suggests that safety concerns over condoms are exaggerated (World Health Organization, 2007).

As discussed in this volume, female inmates also engage in both consensual and nonconsensual sexual activity. For that reason, barrier methods should also be readily available to female inmates for preventing the spread of disease. First, the success of the condom distribution program in New South Wales, Australia, led to widespread distribution of condoms and dental dams. In the United States, both dental dams and condoms should be offered to female inmates who may engage in consensual sexual activity with both other inmates and male staff. In addition, some education should be provided along with the barrier methods so that women understand how to properly use them. Correctional administrators should encourage the use of these methods as part of a larger sex education program. Providing access to dental dams and condoms may lower the risk of STD transmission.

Female inmates also reported sexual victimization by other inmates at rates three times higher than males. The possibility exists that the higher rates of victimization among female inmates are more of a reflection on their willingness to report. However, the sexual victimization of female inmates by other inmates and male staff must be taken seriously.

Finally, one of the health concerns unique to women in prison is the possibility of pregnancy due to both consensual and nonconsensual sexual activity with male staff. Opponents of conjugal visitation programs have argued that the medical care costs associated with pregnancy are one of the many reasons they should not be implemented. However, if correctional administrators embraced condom distribution, these fears may not be realized as female inmates can then control their own reproduction in the event such sexual activity occurs.

Safety Concerns

Correctional administrators are forced to consider not only the health concerns caused by sexual activity in prison, but also the safety concerns brought on by such activity since they are charged with ensuring the safety of both inmates under supervision and staff who work in the facilities. Options do exist however to reduce victimization and the violence associated with sexual behavior in prison.

In 2003, President George W. Bush signed PREA into law to address concerns about sexual assault within correctional facilities (Bureau of Justice Statistics, 2004). PREA required all correctional facilities to compile data on rape and sexual assault, provided funding for research and programs, and created a zero-tolerance policy regarding sexual assaults occurring in the correctional system. Since PREA went into effect, the Bureau of Justice Statistics has provided descriptive data on sexual assaults in correctional facilities, as reported previously in the National Former Prisoner Survey.

Tewksbury and Connor summarized the information available on the characteristics of sexual assault victims in prison that has been collected by Bureau of Justice Statistics annually. In their chapter, they highlighted that research indicates sexual assault victims in prison tend to be young (under the age of thirty-five), new to the prison system, and incarcerated for the first time. These newcomers are naïve to the prison subculture and the norms and values associated with being on the "inside," which leaves them vulnerable to sexual victimization. Furthermore, victims of sexual assault in prison often suffer from mental illness. In both instances, older and more experienced inmates prey on those who are easily manipulated. The inmates exploited by these men may develop consensual sexual relationships with these predators with the expectation of friendship, romance, or safety, but then get assaulted. Other times they may be lured into a dangerous situation within the facility by someone they trust, but then cannot extricate themselves. Regardless of the method of seduction and sexual victimization, certain policy changes could decrease the frequency of occurrence and protect both staff and inmates.

One structural suggestion for reducing sexual victimization involves limiting unsupervised space in a correctional facility, where these types of incidents most frequently occur. A new innovation in correctional architecture called the pod design is one potential design solution. The pod design contains rows of cells (generally two levels) against the borders of the pod with a large communal area in the middle. This open area is supervised by a glass-enclosed "eagle's nest" of guards who can electronically control all the entrances. Allowing the inmates to spend the majority of their time in the communal areas makes controlling and supervising their behavior easier. Rather than being given hidden spaces and corners to participate in assaultive behavior, inmates can be watched from a distance.

While the number of inmates who have a diagnosed mental disorder or illness is high, many inmates are not diagnosed or do report their diagnosis when they enter a facility. The first suggestion is to perform a psychiatric evaluation of all inmates upon their entrance into a facility to ensure proper classification and treatment. Second, once inmates have been diagnosed, those with severe mental illnesses or handicaps can be given proper treatment in a segregated mental health unit. Other individuals with illnesses who can be managed with less supervision can be integrated into smaller general population units where they can still be monitored by correctional staff but mainstreamed with the other inmates.

Staff education also is imperative to decreasing sexual assault within prison walls. Correctional staff needs to be prepared to notice the warning signals for the exploitation of these protected groups, as well as be aware of architectural areas within a facility that could be used for an assault. Further, correctional staff should receive regular training on the acceptable behavior between inmates and inmates and staff, as well as the outlets for inmates to report assaultive behavior. Correctional staff members play a multitude of roles, including disciplinarian, supervisor, and counselor. If inmates feel as if they have been targeted or violated in any form, they need to be able to receive the proper guidance from the staff.

Lastly, one suggestion for reducing violence and sexual victimization involves broadening the opportunities for family and conjugal visitation for inmates and their significant others (beyond married individuals). The empirical research to date has noted numerous positive benefits associated with family and conjugal visitation. For example, family and conjugal visitation programs have been found to improve marital and family stability, while increasing the inmates' ability to maintain ties with family upon release (Hensley et al., 2002) and reducing recidivism (Howser, Grossman, and Macdonald, 1983). Furthermore, some studies have found such programs to act as an effective form of social control within the prison by reducing violence and influencing inmate adjustment to prison (Casey-Acevedo and Bakken, 2001, 2002; Hensley, 2002; Schafer, 1991, 1994; Wooldredge, 1997).

In 2002, Hensley concluded *Prison Sex: Practice and Policy* with calls for additional research into sexual behavior in prison, including additional assessments on the benefits of family and conjugal visitation. As discussed, the most recent research suggests that family and conjugal visitation programs provide a variety of benefits both inside and outside of the prison.

Moreover, the most recent research by D'Alessio and colleagues (2012) on the reduced incidents of sexual violence in prisons that allow conjugal visitation cannot be ignored. Since the publication of *Prison Sex* more than ten years ago, no additional states have allowed conjugal visitation. If the safety and security of both inmates and correctional staff are a priority, then state correctional administrators must consider the results of these findings and find a way to implement these programs that offsets the risks. Although the public favors more punitive strategies in regard to amenities in prison, more support exists among the public for family visitation programs. As is the case in most of the states with conjugal visitation, offering this option as part of a family reunification program that seeks to maintain family ties and stability while incarcerated is possible.

Conclusion

Incarcerating an individual can affect the sexual behaviors and experiences of that individual in a dramatic way—and in turn, that individual's sexual experiences can affect multiple other aspects of that individual's life. Deprivation of liberty and choice can influence decisions that would not normally be made, such as participation in a relationship with a member of the same sex. Physical desires or emotional need for companionship are often obtained in any way possible simply for psychological survival. An inmate may participate in an unsafe sexual relationship due to the lack of protection, increasing the odds of health issues and the spread of disease.

Deprivation of security and autonomy also puts a person in situations in a prison that are unsafe. Due to the overcrowding in prisons, correctional staff cannot effectively supervise all inmates all the time. Many become victims of physical and sexual assault and are forced to participate in unhealthy and unwelcome interactions with other inmates. Furthermore, some inmates become the victims of correctional staff or are the aggressors in this manipulative relationship.

No matter the issue, the presence of sexual behavior in prison is continuous and growing despite its restriction by prison administration. While our corrections systems have chosen to address the reality of many situations, much room still remains for improvement to ensure the safety and health of those offenders under supervision. Legislation, in-house policies, and education are necessary to improve the outlook of the current situation.

References

Abraham, S. (2001). Male rape in US prisons: Cruel and unusual punishment. *Human Rights Brief* 9, no. 1, Br. 5.

Akers, R., Hayner, N., and Grununger, W. (1974). Homosexual and drug behavior in prison: A test of the functional and importation models of the inmate system. *Social Problems* 21: 410–422.

Akers, T. A., Potter, R. H., and Hill, C. V. (2013). *Epidemiological criminology: A public health approach to crime and violence.* San Francisco: Jossey-Bass.

Alarid, L. F. (2000a). Sexual assault and coercion among incarcerated women prisoners: Excerpts from prison letters. *Prison Journal* 80, no. 4: 391–406.

———. (2000b). Sexual orientation perspectives of incarcerated bisexual and gay men: The county jail protective custody experience. *Prison Journal* 80, no. 1: 80–95.

Allen, B., and Bosta, D. (1981). *Games criminals play: How you can profit by knowing them.* Susanville, CA: Rae John.

Altaf, A., Janjua, N., Kristensen, S., Zaidi, N., Memon, A., Hook, E., Vermund, S., and Shah, S. (2009). High-risk behaviors among juvenile prison inmates in Pakistan. *Public Health* 123, no. 7: 470–475.

American Civil Liberties Union. (2004). *Man raped by prison guard receives money damages in ACLU lawsuit.* Retrieved June 1, 2013, from http://www.aclu.org/prisoners-rights/man-raped-prison-guard-receives -money-damages-aclu-lawsuit.

Amnesty International. (1999). *Women in custody.* New York: Amnesty International. Retrieved June 10, 2013, from http://www.amnestyusa.org /pdf/custodyissues.pdf.

Anno, B. J. (1991). *Prison health care: Guidelines for the management of an adequate delivery system*. Chicago: National Commission on Correctional Health Care.

Antonopoulos, G., and Winterdyk, J. (2005). Techniques of neutralizing the trafficking of women. *European Journal of Crime, Criminal Law, and Criminal Justice* 13: 136–147.

Applegate, B. (2001). Penal austerity: Perceived utility, desert, and public attitudes toward prison amenities. *American Journal of Criminal Justice* 25: 253–268.

Austin, J., Fabelo, T., Gunter, A., and McGinnis, K. (2006). *Sexual violence in the Texas prison system*. Washington, DC: JFA Institute.

Awofeso, N., and Naoum, R. (2002). Sex in prisons: A management guide. *Australian Health Review* 25: 149–158

Bales, W. D., and Mears, D. P. (2008). Inmate social ties and the transition to society: Does visitation reduce recidivism? *Journal of Research in Crime and Delinquency* 45, no. 3: 287–321.

Balogh, J. K. (1964). Conjugal visitations in prisons: A sociological perspective. *Federal Probation* (September): 54–58.

Banbury, S. (2004). Coercive sexual behavior in British prisons as reported by adult ex-prisoners. *Howard Journal* 43, no. 2: 113–130.

Barth, T. (2012). Relationships and sexuality of imprisoned men in the German penal system—a survey of inmates in a Berlin prison. *International Journal of Law and Psychiatry* 35, no. 3: 153–158.

Barton, G. (2005). Prisoner sues state over gender rights: Inmate who gets hormone therapy wants sex change, reassignment. *Journal Sentinel*, January 23. Retrieved March 18, 2013, from http://www.jsonline.com/news/wisconsin/181956101.html.

Beck, A. J. (2012). *PREA data collection activities, 2012* (NCJ no. 238640). Washington, DC: US Department of Justice, Office of Justice Programs.

Beck, A. J., and Harrison, P. (2003). *Prison and jail inmates at midyear 2003*. Washington, DC: Bureau of Justice Statistics.

———. (2005). *Sexual violence reported by correctional authorities, 2004* (NCJ no. 210333). Washington, DC: US Department of Justice, Office of Justice Programs.

———. (2006). *Sexual violence reported by correctional authorities, 2005* (NCJ no. 214645). Washington, DC: US Department of Justice.

———. (2007a). *Sexual violence reported by correctional authorities, 2006* (NCJ no. 218914). Washington, DC: US Department of Justice, Office of Justice Programs.

———. (2007b). *Sexual victimization in state and federal prisons reported by inmates, 2007* (NCJ no. 2194414). Washington, DC: US Department of Justice, Office of Justice Programs.

———. (2008). *Sexual victimization in local jails reported by inmates, 2007* (NCJ no. 221946). Washington, DC: US Department of Justice, Office of Justice Programs.

———. (2010). *Sexual victimization in prisons and jails reported by in-*

mates, 2008–09 (NCJ no. 231169). Washington, DC: US Department of Justice, Office of Justice Programs

Beck, A. J., Harrison, P. M., and Adams, D. B. (2007). *Bureau of Justice Statistics special report: Sexual violence reported by correctional authorities, 2006* (NCJ no. 218914). Washington, DC: US Department of Justice, Office of Justice Programs.

Beck, A. J., and Johnson, C. (2012). *Sexual victimization reported by former state prisoners, 2008* (NCJ no. 237363). Washington, DC: US Department of Justice, Office of Justice Programs.

Beckford v. Department of Corrections, 605 F.3d 951 (11th Cir. 2010).

Belknap, J. (2007). *The invisible woman: Gender, crime and justice.* 3rd ed. Belmont, CA: Wadsworth.

Blain, G. (2011). Conjugal visits allowed for inmates and partners in same-sex marriages, civil unions. *New York Daily News,* April 23. Retrieved June 1, 2013, from http://articles.nydailynews.com/2011-04-23/local/29480796_1_conjugal-visits-civil-unions-gay-marriage.

Blight, J. (2000). Transgender inmates. In *Australian Institute of Criminology: Trends and issues in crime and criminal justice,* 1–6. Canberra: Australian Institute of Criminology.

Blumberg, M., and Laster J. (2009). The impact of HIV/AIDS on corrections. In *Prisons and jails: A reader,* edited by R. Tewksbury and D. Dabney, 291–304. New York: McGraw Hill.

Bondesson, U. (1989). *Prisoners in prison societies.* New Brunswick, NJ: Transaction.

Bosworth, M. F. (1999). *Engendering resistance: Agency and power in a woman's prison.* Aldershot, UK: Ashgate

Bowker, L. (1980). *Prison victimization.* New York: Elsevier North Holland.

Brady, K. (2009). *Correctional Corporation of America's Otter Creek Correctional Center.* Honolulu, HI: Community Alliance on Prisons.

Brewer, T. F., Vlahov, D., Taylor, E., Hall, D., Munoz, A., and Polk, B. F. (1988). Transmission of HIV-1 within a statewide prison system. *AIDS* 2, no. 5: 363.

Bureau of Justice Statistics. (2004). *Data collections for the Prison Rape Elimination Act of 2003.* Washington, DC: US Department of Justice, Office of Justice Programs.

———. (2010). *National survey of youth in custody.* Washington, DC: US Department of Justice, Office of Justice Programs.

———. (2012a). *PREA data collection activities, 2012* (NCJ no. 238640). Washington, DC: US Department of Justice, Office of Justice Programs.

———. (2012b). *Report on sexual victimization in prisons and jails.* Review panel on prison rape, national survey of youth in custody. Retrieved June 1, 2013, from http://www.ojp.usdoj.gov/reviewpanel/reviewpanel.htm.

Burks, W. (2012). *Prison closing leaving more than 170 jobless.* WYMT TV 57 Mountain News, April 13. Retrieved October 16, 2012, from http://www.wkyt.com/wymt/home/headlines/Prison_closing_leaving_more_than_170_without_jobs_147379795.html.

Burstein, J. Q. (1977). *Conjugal visits in prison: Psychological and social consequences.* New York: Lexington Books.

Butler, T., and Milner, L. (2003). *The 2001 New South Wales inmates health survey.* Sydney, Australia: Corrections Health Services.

Byrne, J., and Hummer, D. (2008). Examining the impact of institutional culture on prison violence and disorder: An evidence-based review. In *The culture of prison violence,* edited by J. M. Byrne, D. Hummer, and F. Taxman, 40–66. Boston: Pearson.

Calhoun, A. J., and Coleman, H. D. (2002). Female inmates' perspectives on sexual abuse by correctional personnel: An exploratory study. *Women and Criminal Justice* 13, no. 2/3: 101–124.

California Department of Corrections and Rehabilitation. (2013). *Visitation.* Retrieved May 1, 2013, from http://www.cdcr.ca.gov/Visitors/index.html.

California pays $10,000 to settle sex abuse suit brought by transgender prisoner. (2012). *Prison Legal News* 23, no. 2: 43.

Campbell, C. F. (1980). Co-corrections—FCI Fort Worth after three years. In *Co-ed prison,* edited by J. O. Smykla, 83–109. New York: Human Services Press.

Carroll, L. (1974). *Hacks, blacks, and cons.* Lexington, MA: D. C. Heath.

———. (1977). Humanitarian reform and biracial sexual assault in a maximum security prison. *Urban Life* 5, no. 4: 417–437.

Carson, A. E., and Sabol, W. J. (2012). *Prisoners in 2011* (NCJ no. 239808). Washington, DC: US Department of Justice, Office of Justice Programs.

Casey-Acevedo, K., and Bakken, T. (2001). Effects of visitation on women in prison. *International Journal of Comparative and Applied Criminal Justice* 25, no. 1: 49–70.

———. (2002). Visiting women in prison: Who visits and who cares? *Journal of Offender Rehabilitation* 34, no. 3: 67–83.

Centers for Disease Control and Prevention. (2001). *HIV testing and the criminal justice system.* Retrieved June 1, 2013, from http://stacks.cdc.gov/view/cdc/5506/.

———. (2005). *HIV/AIDS surveillance report,* Vol. 17, table 5a. Retrieved from http://www.cdc.gov/hiv/pdf/statistics_2005_HIV_Surveillance_Report_vol_17.pdf.

———. (2008). *HIV/AIDS surveillance report,* Vol. 18, table 5a. Retrieved from http://www.cdc.gov/hiv/surveillance/resources/reports/2006/report/pdf/2006SurveillanceReport.pdf.

———. (2011). *HIV surveillance report,* Vol. 23, table 1a. Retrieved from http://www.cdc.gov/hiv/pdf/statistics_2011_HIV_Surveillance_Report_vol_23.pdf#Page=31.

———. (2012). *HIV surveillance report,* Vol. 22, no. 2, table 1a. http://www.cdc.gov/hiv/topics/surveillance/resources/reports/.

Chen, J. L., Bovée, M. C., and Kerndt, P. R. (2003). Sexually transmitted diseases surveillance among incarcerated men who have sex with men—an opportunity for HIV prevention. *AIDS Education and Prevention* 15, no. 1 (Supplement): 117–126.

Chesney-Lind, M., and Rodriguez, N. (1983). Women under lock and key. *Prison Journal* 63, no. 3: 47–65.

Chonco, N. R. (1989). Sexual assaults among male inmates: A descriptive study. *Prison Journal* 69, no. 1: 72–82.

Claxton, M., Hansen, R. J., and Sinclair, N. (2005). Sexual abuse behind bars. *Detroit News,* May 22–25.

Clemmer, D. (1940). *The prison community.* Boston: Christopher.

———. (1958). *The prison community.* New York: Holt, Rinehart and Winston.

Cochran, J. C. (2012). The ties that bind or the ties that break: Examining the relationship between visitation and prisoner misconduct. *Journal of Criminal Justice* 40, no. 5: 433–440.

Cohen, F. (2011). Transgender prisoners' right of access to medical care in prison. *Correctional Mental Health Report* 13, no. 4: 49–64.

Corlew, K. R. (2006). Congress attempts to shine a light on a dark problem: An in-depth look at the Prison Rape Elimination Act of 2003. *American Journal of Criminal Law* 33, no. 2: 157–190.

Cotton, D. J., and Groth, A. N. (1984). Sexual assault in correctional institutions: Prevention and intervention. In *Victims of sexual aggression: Treatment of children, women and men,* edited by I. R. Stuart, 127–155. New York: Van Nostrand Reinhold.

Cromwell, P., and Thurman, Q. (2003). The devil made me do it: Use of neutralization by shoplifters. *Deviant Behavior* 24: 535–550.

D'Alessio, S. J., Flexon, J., and Stolzenberg, L. (2012). The effect of conjugal visitation on sexual violence in prison. *American Journal of Criminal Justice.* Retrieved June 1, 2013, from http://www.prearesourcecenter.org/sites/default/files/library/theeffectofconjugalvisitation.pdf.

Davis, A. J. (1968). Sexual assaults in the Philadelphia prison system and sheriff's vans. *Trans-Action* 6, no. 2: 8–16.

Dean-Brown, J. (1993). Social meaning in language, curriculum of language, and through language curriculum. In *Language communication and social meaning,* edited by J. E. Alatis, 117–134. Washington, DC: Georgetown University Press.

Dehghan, S. (2011). Iran giving out condoms for criminals to rape us, say jailed activists. *The Guardian,* June 24. Retrieved June 6, 2013, from http://www.guardian.co.uk/world/2011/jun/24/jailed-iran-opposition-activists-rape.

Deitch, M. (2009). The need for prison oversight. *Fact Sheet,* February. Just Detention International. Retrieved June 1, 2013, from http://www.justdetention.org/en/factsheets/The_Need_for_Prison_Oversight.pdf.

Dial, K., and Worley, R. (2008). Crossing the line: A quantitative analysis of inmate boundary violators in a southern prison system. *American Journal of Criminal Justice* 33: 69–84.

Diamond, L. M. (2000). Sexual identity, attractions, and behavior among young sexual-minority women over a 2-year period. *Developmental Psychology* 36: 241–250.

Diaz-Cotto, J. (1996). *Gender, ethnicity and the state: Latina and Latino prison politics.* Albany, NY: SUNY Press.

———. (2010). Gender, sexuality, and family kinship networks. In *Interrupted life: Experiences of incarcerated women in the United States,* edited by R. Solinger, P. C. Johnson, M. L. Raimon, T. Reynolds, and R. Tapia, 131–144. Berkeley: University of California Press.

Dietrich, R., and Graumann, F. (1989). *Language processing in social context.* Amsterdam: North Holland.

Dolan, K., Lowe, D., and Shearer, J. (2004). Evaluation of the condom distribution program in New South Wales prisons, Australia. *Journal of Law, Medicine and Ethics* 32: 124–128.

Donaldson, S. (1993a). *A million jockers, punks, and queens: Sex among male prisoners and its implications for concepts of sexual orientation.* Stop Prisoner Rape. http://spr.igc.org/en/stephendonaldson/doc_01_lecture.html.

———. (1993b), *Prisoner rape education program: Overview for administrators and staff.* Brandon, VT: Safer Society.

———. (2003). Hooking up: Protective pairing for punks. In *Violence in war and peace: An anthology,* edited by N. Scheper-Hughes and P. Bourgois, 348–353. Williston, VT: Blackwell.

Dumond, R. W. (1992). The sexual assault of male inmates in incarcerated settings. *International Journal of the Sociology of Law* 20, no. 20: 135–157.

———. (2000). Inmate sexual assault: The plague that persists. *Prison Journal* 80, no. 4: 407–414.

———. (2003). Confronting America's most ignored crime problem: The Prison Rape Elimination Act of 2003. *Journal of the American Academy of Psychiatry and the Law* 31, no. 3: 354–360.

———. (2006). The impact of prisoner sexual violence: Challenges in implementing public law 108-79—the Prison Rape Elimination Act of 2003. *Notre Dame Law School, Journal of Legislation* 32, no. 2: 142–164.

Du Mont, J., Miller, K. L., and Myhr, T. L. (2003). The role of "real rape" and "real victim" stereotypes in the police reporting practices of sexually assaulted women. *Violence Against Women* 9, no. 4: 466–486.

Edgar, K., O'Donnell, I., and Martin, C. (2003), *Prison violence: The dynamics of conflict, fear and power.* Cullompton, Davon, UK: Willan.

Edney, R. (2004). To keep me safe from harm? Transgender prisoners and the experience of imprisonment. *Deakin Law Review* 9, no. 2: 327–338.

Eigenberg, H. M. (1989). Male rape: An empirical examination of correctional officers' attitudes toward male rape in prison. *Prison Journal* 68, no. 2: 39–56.

———. (1992). Homosexuality in male prisons: Demonstrating the need for a social constructionist approach. *Criminal Justice Review* 17: 219–234.

———. (2000). Correctional officers and their perceptions of homosexuality, rape and prostitution in male prisons. *Prison Journal* 80, no. 4: 415–433.

———. (2002). Prison staff and male rape. In *Prison sex: Practice and policy,* edited by C. Hensley, 49–65. Boulder, CO: Lynne Rienner.

Einat, T. (2009). Inmate harassment and rape: An exploratory study of seven maximum and medium security male prisons in Israel. *International Journal of Offender Therapy and Comparative Criminology* 53, no. 6: 648–664.

———. (2013). Rape and consensual sex in male Israeli prisons: Are there differences with Western prisons? *Prison Journal* 93, no. 1: 80–101.

Einat, T., and Einat, H. (2000). Inmate argot as an expression of prison subculture: The Israeli case. *Prison Journal* 80, no. 3: 309–325.

Einat, T., and Rabinovitz, S. (forthcoming). A warm touch in a cold cell: Inmates' views on conjugal visits in a maximum-security women's prison in Israel. *International Journal of Offender Therapy and Comparative Criminology.*

Fagan, T. J., Wennerstorm, D., and Miller, J. (1996). Sexual assault of male inmates: Prevention, identification and intervention. *Journal of Correctional Health Care* 3, no. 1: 49–65.

Farmer v. Brennan 511 US 825 (1994).

Farrington, D. (1994). *Psychological explanations of crime.* Aldershot, UK: Dartmouth.

Fishman, J. F. (1934). *Sex in prison: Revealing sex conditions in American prisons.* New York: National Library Press.

Fleisher, M. S. (1989). *Warehousing violence.* Newbury Park, CA: Sage.

Fleisher, M. S., and Krienert, J. L. (2009). *The myth of prison rape: Sexual culture in American prisons.* New York: Rowman and Littlefield.

Foley, R. (2010). Wis. inmate rejects women's underwear, insists on sex change. *Minneapolis–St. Paul Star Tribune,* November 10. Retrieved March 18, 2013, from http://www.startribune.com/templates/Print_This _Story?sid=107059208.

Ford, C. (1929). Homosexual practices of institutionalized females. *Journal of Abnormal and Social Psychology* 23: 442–449.

Fox, J. (1984). Women's prison policy, prisoner activism, and the impact of the contemporary feminist movement: A case study. *Prison Journal* 64, no. 2: 15–36.

Gaes, G., and Goldberg, A. (2004). Prison rape: A critical review of the literature. *National Criminal Justice Reference Service,* March 10. Retrieved June 10, 2013, from https://www.ncjrs.gov/pdffiles1/nij /grants/213365.pdf.

Gagnon, J. H., and Simon, W. (1968). The social meaning of prison homosexuality. *Federal Probation* 32, no. 1: 23–29.

Garland, J. T., Morgan, R. D., and Beer, A. M. (2005). Impact of time in prison and security level on inmates' sexual attitude, behavior, and identity. *Psychological Services* 2: 151–162.

Gear, S. (2005). Rules of engagement: Structuring sex and damage in men's prisons and beyond. *Culture, Health and Sexuality* 7, no. 3: 195–208.

George, E. (2010). *A woman doing life: Notes from a prison for women.* New York: Oxford University Press.

Giallombardo, R. (1966). *Society of women: A study of a women's prison.* New York: Valley.

Gibbons, J. (2011). Confronting confinement: A report on the Commission on Safety and Abuse in America's Prisons. *Federal Sentencing Reporter—General Federal Materials* 24, no. 1: 36–41.

Gilligan, J. (2002). How to increase the rate of violence—and why. In *Exploring corrections: A book of readings,* edited by T. Gray, 200–214. Boston: Allyn and Bacon.

Glaze, L. E. (2010). *Correctional populations in the United States, 2009* (NCJ no. 231681). Washington, DC: US Department of Justice, Office of Justice Programs.

Goetting, A. (1982). Conjugal association in prison: Issues and perspectives. *Crime and Delinquency* 28: 52–71.

Goffman, E. (1961). *Asylums: Essays on the social situation of mental patients and other inmates.* Garden City, NY: Anchor.

Gottesdiener, L. (2011). California women prisons: Inmates face sexual abuse, lack of medical care, and unsanitary conditions. *Huffington Post,* August 3. Retrieved January 15, 2013, from http://www.huffington post.com/2011/06/03/california-women-prisons_n_871125.html.

Gray, T., Mays, G. L., and Stohr, M. K. (1995). Inmate needs and programming in exclusively women's jails. *Prison Journal* 75, no. 2: 186–202.

Green, J., Hetherton, J., Heuston, J., Whiteley, C., and Strang, J. (2003). Heterosexual activity of male prisoners in England and Wales. *International Journal of STD and AIDS* 14, no. 4: 248–252.

Greer, K. (2000). The changing nature of interpersonal relationships in a women's prison. *Prison Journal* 80, no. 4: 442–468.

Groth, N. (1979). *Men who rape: The psychology of the offender.* New York: Plenum.

Guerino, P., Harrison, P. M., and Sabol, W. J. (2011). *Prisoners in 2010* (NCJ no. 236096). Washington, DC: US Department of Justice, Office of Justice Programs.

Guillen, J. (2011). Governor Kasich plans to sell prisons, privatize state liquor profits, Turnpike lease could be in near future. *Cleveland Plain Dealer,* March 15. Retrieved October 16, 2012, from http://www.cleveland.com /open/index.ssf/2011/03/gov_kasich_plans_to_sell_priso.html.

Gyarmathy, A., Neaigus, A., and Szamado, S. (2003). HIV risk behavior history of prison inmates in Hungary. *AIDS Education and Prevention* 15, no. 6: 561–569.

Hagemann, O. (2008). Conditions of imprisonment—victimization and conflict in European prisons. *Journal of Ethnicity in Criminal Justice* 6, no. 4: 281–302.

Harm Reduction in Prison Coalition. (2011). *Factsheet 2—AIDS Foundation in Chicago.* Retrieved October 28, 2012, from www.aidschicago.org /pdf/2011/factsheet_2.doc.

Harrison, P. M., and Beck, A. J. (2006). *Prison and jail inmates at midyear 2005* (NCJ no. 213133). Washington, DC: US Department of Justice, Office of Justice Programs.

Hart, J. T. (1971). The Inverse Care Law. *Lancet* 1: 405–412.

Hassine, V. (2010). *Life without parole: Living and dying in prison today.* 5th ed. New York: Oxford University Press.

Haycock, J. (1991). Capital crimes: Suicides in jail. *Death Studies* 15, no. 5: 417–433.

Heffernan, E. (1972). *Making it in prison: The square, the cool, and the life.* New York: Wiley Interscience.

Heffernan, E., and Krippel, E. (1980). A co-ed prison. In *Co-ed prison,* edited by J. O. Smykla, 110–119. New York: Human Services Press.

Heil, P., Harrison, L., English, K., and Ahlmeyer, S. (2009). Is prison sexual offending indicative of community risk? *Criminal Justice and Behavior* 36, no. 9: 892–908.

Hensley, C. (2000a). Attitudes toward homosexuality in a male and female prison: An exploratory study. *Prison Journal* 80, no. 4: 434–441.

———. (2000b). What have we learned from studying prison sex? *Humanity and Society* 24, no. 4: 348–360.

———. (2001). Consensual homosexual activity in male prisons. *Corrections Compendium* 26, no. 1: 1–4.

———. (2002). *Prison sex: Practice and policy.* Boulder, CO: Lynne Rienner.

Hensley, C., Castle, T., and Tewksbury, R. (2003). Inmate-to-inmate sexual coercion in a prison for women. *Journal of Offender Rehabilitation* 37, no. 2: 77–87

Hensley, C., Dumond, R., Tewksbury, R., and Dumond D. (2002). Possible solutions for preventing inmate sexual assault: Examining wardens' beliefs. *American Journal of Criminal Justice* 27, no. 1: 19–34.

Hensley, C., Koscheski, M., and Tewksbury, R. (2003). The impact of institutional factors on officially reported sexual assaults in prisons. *Sexuality and Culture* 7, no. 4: 16–26.

———. (2005). Examining the characteristics of male sexual assault targets in a southern maximum security prison. *Journal of Interpersonal Violence* 20, no. 6: 667–679.

Hensley, C., Rutland, S., and Gray-Ray, P. (2000a). The effects of conjugal visits on Mississippi inmates. *Corrections Compendium* 25, no. 4: 1–3, 20–21.

———. (2000b). Inmate attitudes toward the conjugal visitation program in Mississippi prisons: An exploratory study. *American Journal of Criminal Justice* 25, no. 1: 137–145.

Hensley, C., and Tewksbury, R. (2005a). Wardens' perceptions of inmate fear of sexual assault: A research note. *Prison Journal* 85, no. 2: 198–203.

———. (2005b). Wardens' perceptions of prison sex. *Prison Journal* 85, no. 2: 186–197.

Hensley, C., Tewksbury, R., and Castle, T. (2003). Characteristics of prison sexual assault targets in male Oklahoma correctional facilities. *Journal of Interpersonal Violence* 18, no. 6: 595–606.

Hensley, C., Tewksbury, R., and Koscheski, M. (2001). Masturbation uncovered: Autoeroticism in a female prison. *Prison Journal* 81, no. 4: 491–501.

172 References

————. (2002). The characteristics and motivations behind female prison sex. *Women and Criminal Justice* 13, no. 2/3: 125–139.

Hensley, C., Tewksbury, R., and Wright, J. (2001). Exploring the dynamics of masturbation and consensual same-sex activity within a male maximum security prison. *Journal of Men's Studies* 10, no. 1: 59–71.

Hensley, C., Wright, J., Tewksbury, R., and Castle, T. (2003). The evolving nature of the prison argot and sexual hierarchies. *Prison Journal* 83, no. 3: 289–300.

Hess, A. (2010). We know the way to end prison rape. Is it too expensive? *Afropunk,* April 25. http://www.afropunk.com/forum/topics/victims-of -prison-rape-discuss.

Holt, N., and Miller, D. (1972). *Explorations in inmate-family relationships.* Sacramento: California Department of Corrections.

Hopper, C. B. (1962). The conjugal visit at Mississippi state penitentiary. *Journal of Criminal Law, Criminology, and Police Science* 53, no. 3: 340–343.

————. (1969). *Sex in prison: The Mississippi experiment with conjugal visitation.* Baton Rouge: Louisiana State University Press

Horsburgh, C. R., Jr., Jarvis, J. Q., McArther, T., Ignacio, T., and Stock, P. (1990). Seroconversion to human immunodeficiency virus in prison inmates. *American Journal of Public Health* 80, no. 2: 209–210.

Howser, J., Grossman, J., and MacDonald, D. (1983). Impact of family reunion programs on institutional discipline. *Journal of Sociology and Social Welfare* 8: 27–36.

Huggins, D., Capeheart, L., and Newman, E. (2006). Deviants or scapegoats. *Prison Journal* 86, no. 1: 114–139.

Hulin, R., Sr. (2001). Case history of Rodney Hulin. *No escape: Male rape in U.S. prisons.* New York: Human Rights Watch. Retrieved June 1, 2002, from http://www.hrw.org/reports/2001/prison/rodney_hulin.html.

Human Rights Watch. (1996). *All too familiar: Sexual abuse of women in U.S. state prisons.* New York: Human Rights Watch.

————. (2001). *No escape: Male rape in U.S. prisons.* New York: Human Rights Watch.

————. (2003). *Ill equipped: U.S. prisons and offenders with mental illness.* New York: Human Rights Watch.

Ibrahim, A. (1974). Deviant sexual behavior in men's prisons. *Crime and Delinquency* 20, no. 1: 38–44.

Irwin, J. (1980). *Prisons in turmoil.* Boston: Little, Brown.

Irwin, J., and Cressey, D. R. (1962). Thieves, convicts and the inmate culture. *Social Problems* 10, no. 2: 142–155.

Jafa, K., McElroy, P., Fitzpatrick, L., Borkowf, C. B., MacGowan, R., Margolis, A., Robbins, K., Youngpairoj, A. S., Stratford, D., Greenberg, A., Taussig, J., Shouse, R. L., Lamarre, M., McLellan-Lemal, E., Heneine, W., and Sullivan, P. S. (2009). HIV transmission in a state prison system, 1988–2005. *PLOS One* 4, no. 5.

Jenness, V., Maxson, C. L., Matsuda, K. N., and Sumner, J. (2007). *Violence in California correctional facilities: An empirical examination of sexual assault*. Sacramento: California Department of Corrections and Rehabilitation.

Jenness, V., Maxson, C. L., Sumner, J. M., and Matsuda, K. N. (2010). Accomplishing the difficult, but not impossible: Collecting self-report data on inmate-on-inmate sexual assault in prison. *Criminal Justice Policy Review* 21, no. 1: 3–30.

Johnsrud, S. (2010). *Survivor stories*. Stop Prison Rape. http://spr.igc.org/en/survivorstories/stevenmn.html.

Jones, R. S. (1993). Coping with separation: Adaptive responses of women prisoners. *Women and Criminal Justice* 5, no. 1: 71–96.

Jones, R. S., and Schmid, T. J. (1989). Inmates' conceptions of prison sexual assault. *Prison Journal* 69, no. 1: 53–61.

———. (2000). *Doing time: Prison experience and identity*. Stanford, CT: JAI.

Just Detention International. (2009). Incarcerated youth at extreme risk of sexual abuse. *Fact Sheet,* January. Retrieved June 1, 2013, from http://www.justdetention.org/en/factsheets/jdifactsheetyouth.pdf.

Kahn, R. H., Scholl, D. T., Shane, S. M., Lemoine, A. L., and Farley, T. A. (2002). Screening for syphilis in arrestees: Usefulness for community-wide syphilis surveillance and control. *Sexually Transmitted Diseases* 29, no. 3: 150–156.

Kahn, R. H., Voigt, R. F., Swint, E., and Weinstock, H. (2004). Early syphilis in the United States identified in corrections facilities, 1999–2002. *Sexually Transmitted Diseases* 31, no. 6: 360–364.

Kaiser, D., and Stannow, L. (2010). Prison rape: Eric Holder's unfinished business. *New York Review of Books,* August 26. Retrieved June 1, 2013, from http://www.nybooks.com/blogs/nyrblog/2010/aug/26/prison-rape-holders-unfinished-business/.

———. (2012). Prison rape: Obama's program to stop it. *New York Review of Books,* October 11. http://www.nybooks.com/articles/archives/2012/oct/11/prison-rape-obamas-program-stop-it/.

Kaminski, M. M. (2003). Games prisoners play: Allocation of social roles in a total institution. *Rationality and Society* 15, no. 2: 188–217.

Kang, S.-Y., Deren, S., Andia, J., Colón, H., Robles, R., and Oliver-Velez, D. (2005). HIV transmission behaviors in jail/prison among Puerto Rican drug injectors in New York and Puerto Rico. *AIDS and Behavior* 9, no. 3: 377–386.

Kasdan, D. (2010). Florida court upholds right of pregnant woman to determine medical care. *ACLU Newsletter,* August 12. Retrieved June 1, 2013, from http://www.aclu.org/reproductive-freedom/florida-court-upholds-right-pregnant-woman-determine-medical-care.

Kent, N. E. (1975). Legal and sociological dimensions of conjugal visitation in prisons. *New England Journal on Prison Law* 2, no. 1: 47–65.

Kerr, T., Wood, E., Betteridge, G., Lines, R., and Jürgens, R. (2004). Harm reduction in prisons: A "rights based analysis." *Critical Public Health* 14, no. 4: 345–360.

Keys, D. P. (2002). Instrumental sexual scripting: An examination of gender-role fluidity in the correctional institution. *Journal of Contemporary Criminal Justice* 18, no. 3: 258–278.

Kirkham, G. (1971). Homosexuality in prison. In *Studies in the sociology of sex,* edited by J. M. Henslin, 325–344. New York: Appleton-Century-Crofts.

Koscheski, M., and Hensley, C. (2001). Inmate homosexual behavior in a southern female correctional facility. *American Journal of Criminal Justice* 25, no. 2: 269–277.

Koscheski, M., Hensley, C., Wright, J., and Tewksbury, R. (2002). Consensual sexual behavior. In *Prison sex: Practice and policy,* edited by C. Hensley, 111–131. Boulder, CO: Lynne Rienner.

Krebs, C. P. (2006). Inmate factors associated with HIV transmission in prison. *Criminology and Public Policy* 5, no. 1: 101–124.

Krebs, C. P., and Simmons, M. (2002). Intraprison HIV transmission: An assessment of whether it occurs, how it occurs, and who is at risk. *AIDS Education and Prevention* 14, no. 5 (Supplement): 53–64.

Laumann, E. O., Gagnon, J. H., Michael, R. T., and Michaels, S. (1994). *The social organization of sexuality: Sexual practices in the United States.* Chicago: University of Chicago Press.

Lavoie, D. (2012). Michelle Kosilek, inmate born as Robert Kosilek, eligible for legal fees reimbursement in addition to sex change. *Huffington Post,* September 17. Retrieved March 18, 2013, from http://www.huffington post.com/2012/09/17/michelle-kosilek-inmate-robert-kosilek-legal-fees -sex-change_n_1890043.html.

Leach, D. L. (2007). Issues surrounding managing lesbian, gay, bisexual, transsexual, and intersex (LGBTI) offenders in jails. *American Jails,* November/December, 77–81.

Levan, K., Polzer, K., and Downing, S. (2011). Media and prison sexual assault: How we got to the "don't drop the soap" culture. *International Journal of Criminology and Sociological Theory* 4: 674–682.

Lipscomb, G. H., Muram, D., Speck, P. M., and Mercer, B. M. (1992). Male victims of sexual assault. *Journal of the American Medical Association* 267, no. 22: 3064–3066.

Listwan, S. J., and Hanley, D. (2012). *The prison experience and reentry: Examining the impact of victimization on coming home.* Washington, DC: National Institute of Justice.

Lockwood, D. (1980). *Prison sexual violence.* New York: Elsevier.

MacKenzie, D. L., Robinson, J. W., and Campbell, C. S. (1989). Long-term incarceration of female offenders. *Criminal Justice and Behavior* 16: 223–238.

Maitland, A. S., and Sluder, R. D. (1996). Victimization in prisons: A study of factors related to the general well-being of youthful inmates. *Federal Probation* 60, no. 2: 24–31.

———. (1998). Victimization and youthful prison inmates: An empirical analysis. *Prison Journal* 78, no. 1: 55–73.

Man, C., and Cronan, J. P. (2002). Forecasting sexual abuse in prison: The prison subculture of masculinity as a backdrop for "deliberate indiffer-ence." *Journal of Criminal Law and Criminology* 92, no. 127: 1–17.

Marcum, C. D., Hilinski, C., and Freiburger, T. (forthcoming). Examining the correlates of male and female inmate misconduct. *Security Journal.*

Marquart, J. W., Barnhill, M. B., and Balshaw-Biddle, K. (2001). Fatal at-traction: An analysis of employee boundary violations in a southern prison system, 1995–1998. *Justice Quarterly* 18: 878–910.

Marquart, J. W., Merianos, D. E., Cuvelier, S. J., and Carroll, L. (1996). Thinking about the relationship between health dynamics in the free community and the prison. *Crime and Delinquency* 42, no. 3: 331–360.

Maruschak, L. M. (2009). *HIV in prisons, 2007–08* (NCJ no. 228307). Washington, DC: Office of Justice Programs: US Department of Justice.

———. (2012). *HIV in prisons, 2001–2010* (NCJ no. 238877). Washington, DC: Office of Justice Programs: US Department of Justice.

Mauer, M. (2013). *Incarceration*. Retrieved January 15, 2013, from http://www.sentencingproject.org/detail/news.cfm?news_id=1519&id=167.

May, J. P., and Williams, E. L. (2002). Acceptability of condom availability in a US jail. *AIDS Education and Prevention* 14, no. 5 (Supplement: *HIV/AIDS in Correctional Settings*): 85–91.

McClure, L. (2008). Sex and the slammer. *Mother Jones* 33, no. 4: 60.

McConnell, E. H. (1999). Are conjugal and familial visitations effective re-habilitative concepts? *Prison Journal* 79, no. 1: 124–131.

McGuire, M. D. (2011). Doing the life: An exploration of the connection be-tween the inmate code and violence among female inmates. *Journal of the Institute of Justice and International Studies* (University of Central Missouri, Institute of Justice and International Studies). Retrieved June 13, 2013, from http://www.highbeam.com/doc/1P3-2509399651.html.

McKinley, J. (2007). California to permit conjugal visits for gay inmates. *New York Times,* June 3. Retrieved June 1, 2013, from http://www.ny times.com/2007/06/03/world/americas/03iht-conjugal.1.5975371.html.

Merotte, L. (2012). Sexuality in prison: Three investigation methods analy-sis. *Sexologies* 21, no. 3: 122–125.

Mississippi Department of Corrections. (2013). *Conjugal visits.* Retrieved May 1, 2013, from http://www.mdoc.state.ms.us/conjugal_visits.htm.

Mitchell, K. (2005). 5 prison officers face charges, three accused of having sex with female inmates; warden quits. *Denver Post,* February 25, p. B5.

Money, J., and Bohmer, C. (1980). Prison sexology: Two personal accounts of masturbation, homosexuality, and rape. *Journal of Sex Research* 16: 258–266.

Morris, R., and Higgins, G. (2009). Neutralizing potential and self-reported digital piracy: A multitheoretical exploration among college undergrad-uates. *Criminal Justice Review* 34: 173–195.

Moss, C. S., Hosford, R. E., and Anderson, W. R. (1979). Sexual assault in prison. *Psychological Reports* 44: 823–828.

Moster, A. N., and Jeglic, E. L. (2009). Prison warden attitude toward prison rape and sexual assault: Findings since the Prison Rape Elimination Act (PREA). *Prison Journal* 89, no. 1: 65–78.

Murphy, D. (2012). *Corrections and post-traumatic stress symptoms.* Durham, NC: Carolina Academic Press.

Nacci, P. L. (1978). A federal study: Sexual assault in prisons. *American Journal of Corrections* 40, no. 1: 30–31.

Nacci, P. L., and Kane, T. R. (1983). The incidence of sex and sexual aggression in federal prisons. *Federal Probation* 47, no. 4: 31–36.

———. (1984a). Sex and sexual aggression in federal prisons: Inmate involvement and employee impact. *Federal Probation* 48, no. 1: 46–53.

———. (1984b). Inmate sexual aggression: Some evolving propositions, empirical findings, and mitigating counter-forces. *Journal of Offender Counseling, Services and Rehabilitation* 9, no. 1–2: 1–20.

National Institute of Allergy and Infectious Diseases. (2001). *Workshop summary: Scientific evidence on condom effectiveness for sexually transmitted disease (STD) prevention.* Hernon, VA: National Institutes of Health, Department of Health and Human Services.

National Institute of Corrections. (2000). *Sexual misconduct in prisons: Law, remedies, and incidence.* Washington, DC: US Department of Justice, National Institute of Corrections.

———. (2006). *Staff perspectives: Sexual violence in adult prisons and jails: Investigations.* Washington, DC: US Department of Justice, National Institute of Corrections.

Nerenberg, R. (2002). Spotlight: Condoms in correctional settings. *The body: The complete HIV/AIDS resource.* Retrieved June 1, 2013, from www.thebody.com/content/art13017.html.

Neuman, W. L. (1997). *Social research methods: Qualitative and quantitative approaches.* 3rd ed. Boston: Allyn and Bacon.

New York State Department of Corrections and Community Supervision. (2013). Ministerial, family and volunteer services. Retrieved May 1, 2013, from http://www.doccs.ny.gov/ProgramServices/ministerial.html.

Niehaus, I. (2002). Renegotiating masculinity in the South African Lowveld: Narratives of male-male sex in labor compounds and in male prisons. *African Studies* 61, no. 1: 77–97.

Obama, B. (2012). *Presidential memorandum—implementing the Prison Rape Elimination Act,* May 17. Retrieved October 16, 2012, from http://www.whitehouse.gov/the-press-office/2012/05/17/presidential-memorandum-implementing-prison-rape-elimination-act.

Office of the Inspector General. (2005). *Deterring staff sexual abuse of federal inmates.* Washington, DC: US Department of Justice.

Okochi, C., Oladepo, O., and Ajuwon, A. (1999–2000). Knowledge about AIDS and sexual behaviors of inmates of Agodi Prison in Ibadan, Nigeria. *International Quarterly of Community Health Education* 19, no. 4: 353–364.

Otis, M. (1913). A perversion not commonly noted. *Journal of Abnormal Psychology* 8: 113–116.

Owen, B. A. (1998). *"In the mix": Struggle and survival in a women's prison.* Albany, NY: SUNY Press.

Owen, B., and Moss, A. (2009). Sexual violence in women's prisons and jails: Results from focus group interviews. In *Staff perspectives: Sexual violence in adult prisons and jails,* vol. 3 (1–20). Washington, DC: National Institute of Corrections.

Owen, B., and Wells, J. W. (2006). *Staff perspectives: Sexual violence in adult prisons and jails,* vol. 1. Washington, DC: National Institute of Corrections.

Owen, B., Wells, J., Pollock, J., Muscat, B., and Torres, S. (2008). *Gendered violence and safety: A contextual approach to improving security in women's facilities.* Washington, DC: National Institute of Justice, US Department of Justice, Office of Justice Programs.

Pardue, A., Arrigo, B. A., and Murphy, D. S. (2011). Sex and sexuality in women's prisons: A preliminary typological investigation. *Prison Journal* 91, no. 3: 279–304.

Parenti, C. (2003) Guarding their silence. In *Prison nation: The warehousing of America's poor,* edited by T. Herivel and P. Wright, 252–257. New York: Routledge.

Paris, J., and LaMarre, M. (2006). What are the implications of the results of the study conducted in the Georgia Department of Corrections for HIV prevention in prisons? *Infectious Diseases in Corrections Report* 9, no. 5: 4–5.

Petersen, M., Stephens, J., Dickey, R., and Lewis, W. (1996). Transsexuals within the prison system: An international survey of correctional services policies. *Behavioral Sciences and the Law* 14: 219–229.

Pew Center. (2008). *Pew report finds more than one in 100 adults are behind bars.* Press release of the Public Safety Performance Project, February 28. Retrieved June 1, 2013, from http://www.pewcenteronthe states.org/news_room_detail.aspx?id=35912.

Pollock, J. M. (1998). *Criminal women.* Cincinnati, OH: Anderson.

———. (2002). *Women, prison, and crime.* 2nd ed. Belmont, CA: Wadsworth.

Pollock-Byrne, J. M. (1990). *Women, prison, and crime.* Belmont, CA: Wadsworth.

Potter, R. H. (2007). Why jails are important to community health. *American Jails Magazine* 21 no. 5: 41–43.

Potter, R. H., and Krider, J. E. (2000). Teaching about violence prevention: A bridge between public health and criminal justice educators. *Journal of Criminal Justice Education* 11: 339–351.

Potter, R. H., Lin, H., Maze, A., and Bjoring D. (2011). The health of jail inmates: The role of jail population "flow" in community health. *Criminal Justice Review* 36, no. 4: 470–486.

Potter, R. H., and Rosky, J. (2013). The iron fist in the latex glove: The intersection of public health and criminal justice. *American Journal of Criminal Justice* 38, no. 2: 276–288.

Potter, R. H., and Tewksbury, R. (2005). Sex and prisoners: Criminal justice contributions to a public health issue. *Journal of Correctional Health Care* 11, no. 2: 170–190.

Power, K., Markova, I., Rowlands, A., McKee, K., Anslow, P., and Kilfedder, C. (1991). Sexual behavior in Scottish prisons. *British Medical Journal* 302: 1507–1508.

Prendergast, A. (2006). If the shoe fits: Did Colorado prison guards look the other way while a guard's fetish turned violent? *Prison Legal News* (February).

———. (2011). Raped and extorted by a prison gang, Scott Howard was called a "drama queen" by corrections officials. *Denver Westword News,* February 2. http://www.westword.com/2011-02-03/news/211 -crew-rapes-extorts-scott-howard-colorado-prison.

Prison Rape Elimination Act of 2003. Pub. L. No. 108-79. 117 Stat. 972 (2003).

Propper, A. M. (1978). Lesbianism in female and coed correctional institutions. *Journal of Homosexuality* 3: 265–274.

———. (1981). *Prison homosexuality.* Lexington, MA: S. C. Health.

———. (1982). Make-believe families and homosexuality among imprisoned girls. *Criminology* 20, no. 1: 127–138.

Rennison, C. M. (2002). *Rape and sexual assault: Reporting to police and medical attention, 1992–2000* (NCJ no. 194530). Washington, DC: Office of Justice Programs.

Richey, W. (2012). Supreme Court lets stand ruling that sides with transgender inmates. *Christian Science Monitor,* March 26. Retrieved March 18, 2013, from http://www.csmonitor.com/USA/Justice/2012/0326 /Supreme-Court-lets-stand-ruling-that-sides-with-transgender-inmates.

Richters, J., Butler, T., Schneider, K., Yap, L., Kirkwood, K., Grant, L., Richards, A., Smith, A. M., and Donovan, B. (2012). Consensual sex between men and sexual violence in Australian prisons. *Archives in Sexual Behavior* 41, no. 2: 517–524.

Robertson, J. E. (1999). Cruel and unusual punishment in the United States: Sexual harassment in male prisons. *American Criminal Law Review* 36: 1–44.

Robinson, R. K. (2011). Masculinity as prison: Sexual identity, race, and incarceration. *California Law Review* 99: 1309–1321.

Ross, J., and Richards, S. (2002). *Behind bars: Surviving prison.* Indianapolis, IN: Alpha.

Ross, R. R., and Fabiano, E. A. (1986). *Female offenders: Correctional afterthoughts.* Jefferson, NC: McFarland.

Rotily, M., Galinier-Pujol, A., and Vernay-Vaisse, C. (1995). Risk behaviors of inmates in south-eastern France. *AIDS Care* 1: 89–93.

Ruback, B. (1980). The sexually integrated prison. In *Co-ed prison,* edited by J. O. Smykla, 33–60. New York: Human Services Press.

Sagarin, E. (1976). Prison homosexuality and its effect on post-prison behavior. *Psychiatry* 39: 245–257.

Santos, M. (2008). Prison culture: Are you a convict or an inmate? *Prison*

News Blog—Prison News and Commentary, December 7. Retrieved June 1, 2013, from http://prisonnewsblog.com/2008/12/are-you-a-convict-or-an-inmate/.

Saum, C. A., Surratt, H. L., Inciardi, J. A., and Bennett, R. E. (1995). Sex in prison: Exploring the myths and realities. *Prison Journal* 75, no. 4: 413–430.

Schafer, N. E. (1991). Prison visiting policies and practices. *International Journal of Offender Therapy and Comparative Criminology* 35: 263–275.

———. (1994). Exploring the link between visits and parole success: A survey of prison visitors. *International Journal of Offender Therapy and Comparative Criminology* 38: 17–32.

Selling, L. (1931). The pseudo-family. *American Journal of Sociology* 37: 247–253.

Severance, T. A. (2005). The prison lesbian revisited. *Journal of Gay and Lesbian Social Services* 17, no. 3: 39–57.

Sexton, L., Jenness, V., and Sumner, J. M. (2010). Where the margins meet: A demographic assessment of transgender inmates in men's prisons. *Justice Quarterly* 27, no. 6: 835–866.

Singh, S. (2007). Being a criminology ethnographer in a South African prison: A search for dynamics and prevalence of HIV/AIDS in the Westville prison, Durban, South Africa. *Journal of Social Science* 15, no. 1: 71–82.

Smith, B. V. (2008). The Prison Rape Elimination Act: Implementation and unresolved issues. *Criminal Law Brief* 3, no. 2: 10–18.

Smith, N. E., and Batiuk, M. E. (1989). Sexual victimization and inmate social interaction. *Prison Journal* 69, no. 2: 29–38.

Stinchcomb, J. B. (2011). *Corrections: Foundations for the future.* 2nd ed. New York: Routledge.

Stop Prisoner Rape. (2003). *The sexual abuse of female inmates in Ohio.* Los Angeles: Stop Prisoner Rape.

———. (2006). *In the shadows: Sexual violence in U.S. detention facilities.* Los Angeles: Stop Prisoner Rape.

Stop Prisoner Rape and American Civil Liberties Union National Prison Project. (2005). *Still in danger: The ongoing threat of sexual violence against transgender prisoners.* Los Angeles: Stop Prisoner Rape and American Civil Liberties Union.

Stöver H., ed. (2001). *An overview study: Assistance to drug users in European Union prisons.* Lisbon, Portugal: European Monitoring Centre for Drugs and Drug Addiction.

Struckman-Johnson, C., and Struckman-Johnson, D. (2000). Sexual coercion rates in seven midwestern prison facilities for men. *Prison Journal* 80, no. 4: 379–390.

———. (2002). Sexual coercion reported by women in three midwestern prisons. *Journal of Sex Research* 39, no. 3: 217–227.

———. (2006). A comparison of sexual coercion experiences reported by men and women in prison. *Journal of Interpersonal Violence* 21, no. 12: 1591–1615.

Struckman-Johnson, C., Struckman-Johnson, D., Rucker, L., Bumby, K., and Donaldson, S. (1996). Sexual coercion reported by men and women in prison. *Journal of Sex Research* 33, no. 1: 67–76.

Sykes, G. M. (1958). *The society of captives: A study of maximum security prison.* Princeton, NJ: Princeton University Press.

Sylla, M., Harawa, N., and Reznick, O. G. (2010). The first condom machine in a U.S. jail: The challenge of harm reduction in a law and order environment. *American Journal of Public Health* 100, no. 6: 982–985.

Tarzwell, S. (2006). The gender lines are marked with razor wire: Addressing state prison policies and practices for the management of transgender prisoners. *Columbia Human Rights Law Review* 38: 167–219.

Tewksbury, R. (1989a). Measures of sexual behavior in an Ohio prison. *Sociology and Social Research* 74, no. 1: 34–39.

———. (1989b). Fear of sexual assault in prison inmates. *Prison Journal* 69, no. 1: 62–71.

Tewksbury, R., and Mustaine, E. E. (2005). Insiders' views of prison amenities: Beliefs and perceptions of correctional staff members. *Criminal Justice Review* 30, no. 2: 174–188.

Tewksbury, R., and West, A. (2000). Research on sex in prison in the late 1980s and early 1990s. *Prison Journal* 80, no. 4: 368–378.

Texas Department of Criminal Justice. (2006). *Texas Department of Criminal Justice statistical report 2005.* Austin: Texas Department of Criminal Justice.

Thomas, C. W. (1977). Theoretical perspective on prisonization: A comparison of the importation and deprivation models. *Journal of Criminal Law and Criminology* 68: 135–145.

Thompson, R. A., Nored, L. S., and Dial, K. C. (2008). The Prison Rape Elimination Act (PREA): An evaluation of policy compliance with illustrative excerpts. *Criminal Justice Policy Review* 19, no. 4: 414–437.

Thornhill, R., and Palmer, C. T. (2000). *A natural history of rape: Biological bases of sexual coercion.* Cambridge, MA: MIT Press.

Toch, H. (1977). *Living in prison: The ecology of survival.* New York: Free Press.

———. (1992). *Mosaic of despair.* Washington, DC: American Psychological Association.

Trammell, R. (2011). Symbolic violence and prison wives: Gender roles and protective pairing in men's prisons. *Prison Journal* 91, no. 3: 305–324.

———. (2012). *Enforcing the convict code: Violence and prison culture.* Boulder, CO: Lynne Rienner.

Urbina, I. (2009). Hawaii to remove inmates over abuse charges. *New York Times,* August 26. Retrieved June 1, 2013, from http://www.nytimes.com/2009/08/26/us/26kentucky.html?_r=0.

US Department of Health and Human Services. (2007). *Sexually transmitted disease surveillance 2006,* tables 11B, 21B, 33B. http://www.cdc.gov/std/stats06/pdf/Surv2006.pdf.

————. (2011). *Sexually transmitted disease surveillance 2010,* tables 22B, 11B, 35B. http://www.cdc.gov/std/stats10/surv2010.pdf.

————. (2012). *Sexually transmitted disease surveillance 2011,* tables 22B, 35B, 11B. http://www.cdc.gov/std/stats11/Surv2011.pdf.

US General Accounting Office. (1999). *Women in prisons: Sexual misconduct by correctional staff.* Washington, DC: US General Accounting Office.

Vielmetti, B. (2012). U.S. Supreme Court rejects Wisconsin bid to ban transgender inmate treatments. *Journal Sentinel,* March 26. Retrieved March 18, 2013, from http://www.jsonline.com/news/wisconsin /us-supreme-court-rejects-wisconsin-bid-to-ban-transgender-inmate -treatments-144o1ie-144222455.html.

Von Zielauer, P. (2005). New York set to close jail unit for gays. *New York Times,* December 30. Retrieved March 18, 2013, from http://www .nytimes.com/2005/12/30/nyregion/30jails.html.

Walmsley, R. (2009). *World prison population list.* 8th ed. Washington, DC: US Department of Justice, National Institute of Corrections.

Ward, D. A., and Kassebaum, G. G. (1964). Homosexuality: A mode of adaptation in a prison for women. *Social Problems* 12: 159–177.

————. (1965). *Women's prison: Sex and social structure.* Chicago: Aldine.

Warner, L., Stone, K. M., Macaluso, M., Buehler, J. W., and Austin, H. D. (2006). Condom use and risk of gonorrhea and chlamydia: A systematic review of design and measurement factors assessed in epidemiologic studies. *Sexually Transmitted Diseases* 33: 36–51.

Washington State Department of Corrections. (2013). *Extended family visits.* Retrieved May 1, 2013, from http://www.doc.wa.gov/family/extended familyvisits.asp.

Watterson, K. (1996). *Women in prison: Inside the concrete womb.* Rev. ed. Boston: Northeastern University Press.

Welch, M. (1996). *Corrections: A critical approach.* New York: McGraw-Hill.

Weild, A., Gill, O., Bennett, D., Livingstone, S., Parry, J., and Curran, L. (2000). Prevalence of HIV, hepatitis B, and hepatitis C antibodies in prisoners in England and Wales: A national survey. *Communicable Disease and Public Health* 3, no. 2: 121–126.

Whittle, S., and Stephens, P. (2001). *A pilot study of provision for transsexual and transgender people in the criminal justice system, and the information needs of their probation officers.* Manchester, UK: Manchester Metropolitan University.

Wilkinson, R. A. (2003a). The cost of conjugal visitation outweighs the benefits. *Corrections Today* 65, no. 3: 19–20.

————. (2003b). Sexuality and corrections: An administrator's perspective. *Sexuality and Culture* 7, no. 4: 11–15.

Williams, S. P., and Kahn, R. H. (2007). Looking inside and affecting the outside: Corrections-based interventions for STD prevention. In *Behavioral interventions for prevention and control of sexually transmitted diseases,* edited by S. O. Aral and J. M. Douglas, 374–396. New York: Springer Science and Business Media.

Willis, A. K., and Zaitzow, B. H. (2010). Doing "life": A glimpse into the long-term incarceration experience. Paper presented at the American Society of Criminology meeting, San Francisco, November 17–20.

Wolff, N., Blitz, C. L., and Shi, J. (2007). Rates of sexual victimization in prison for inmates with and without mental disorders. *Psychiatric Services* 58, no. 8: 1087–1094.

Wolff, N., Blitz, C. L., Shi, J., Bachman, R., and Siegel, J. A. (2006). Sexual violence inside prisons: Rates of victimization. *Journal of Urban Health* 83, no. 5: 835–848.

Wolff, N., and Shi, J. (2008). Patterns of victimization and feelings of safety inside prison: The experience of male and female inmates. *Crime and Delinquency* 57, no. 1: 29–55.

———. (2009). Type, source, and patterns of physical victimization: A comparison of male and female inmates. *Prison Journal* 89, no. 2: 172–191.

Wolff, N., Shi, J., Blitz, C. L., and Siegel, J. A. (2007). Understanding sexual victimization inside prisons: Factors that predict risk. *Criminology and Public Policy* 6, no. 3: 535–564.

Wooden, W., and Parker, J. (1982). *Men behind bars: Sexual exploitation in prison.* New York: Plenum.

Wooldredge, J. D. (1991). Correlates of deviant behavior among inmates in U.S. correctional facilities. *Journal of Crime and Justice* 14, no. 1: 1–25.

———. (1997). Explaining variation in perceptions of inmate crowding. *Prison Journal* 77, no. 1: 27–40.

Wooldredge, J. D., and Steiner, B. (2009). Comparing methods for examining relationships between prison crowding and inmate violence. *Justice Quarterly* 26, no. 4: 795–826.

World Health Organization. (2007). *Evidence of interventions to manage HIV in prison—provision of condoms and other measures to decrease sexual victimization.* Retrieved October 21, 2012, from http://www.who.int/hiv/idu/Prisons_condoms.pdf.

Worley, R. M., and Cheeseman, K. A. (2006). Guards as embezzlers: The consequences of "nonshareable" problems in prison settings. *Deviant Behavior* 27: 203–222.

Worley, R., Marquart, J., and Mullings, J. (2003). Prison guard predators: An analysis of inmates who established inappropriate relationships with prison staff, 1995–1998. *Deviant Behavior* 24: 175–194.

Worley, R., and Worley, V. B. (2013). Inmate public autoerotism uncovered: Exploring the dynamics of masturbatory behavior within correctional facilities. *Deviant Behavior* 34: 11–24.

Yap, L., Butler, T., Richters, J., Kirkwood, K., Grant, L., Saxby, M., Ropp, F., and Donovan, B. (2007). Do condoms cause rape and mayhem? The long-term effects of condoms in New South Wales' prisons. *Sexually Transmitted Infections* 3: 219–222.

Yap, L., Richters, J., Butler, T., Schneider, K., Grant, L., and Donovan, B. (2011). The decline in sexual assaults in men's prisons in New South Wales: A "systems" approach. *Journal of Interpersonal Violence* 26, no. 15: 3157–3181.

Zaitzow, B. H. (1999). Doing time: Everybody's doing it. *Criminal Justice Policy Review* 9, no. 1: 13–42.

———. (2003). "Doing gender" in a women's prison. In *Women in prison: Gender and social control,* edited by B. H. Zaitzow and J. Thomas, 21–38. Boulder, CO: Lynne Rienner.

———. (2008). Uniformed abusers: Officer misconduct against women prisoners. Paper presented at the American Society of Criminology meeting, St. Louis, MO, November 12–15, 2008.

The Contributors

Ashley G. Blackburn is assistant professor in the Department of Criminal Justice at the University of Houston. She has published corrections-related research in such journals as *Prison Journal, Journal of Offender Rehabilitation, Journal of Criminal Justice,* and *Deviant Behavior.* Recently she coedited *Prisons: Today and Tomorrow,* 3rd ed. (with Shannon K. Fowler and Joycelyn M. Pollock).

Tammy L. Castle is associate professor in the Department of Justice Studies at James Madison University. She has published broadly in the area of sexual violence and prisons in *Prison Journal, Journal of Offender Rehabilitation,* and *Journal of Interpersonal Violence.*

David P. Connor is a doctoral student in the Department of Justice Administration at the University of Louisville. His research interests include sex offenders and sex offenses, institutional corrections, and inmate reentry. His most recent publications have appeared in *Federal Probation, Journal of Crime and Justice,* and *Western Criminology Review.*

Tomer Einat is lecturer in the Department of Criminology at Bar Ilan University. His major areas of research are penology, male and female prisons, same-sex sexual relations among male and female prisoners, alternatives to incarceration, criminal justice, and learning disabilities and criminal behavior.

Shannon L. Fowler is assistant professor, assistant chair, and graduate coordinator in the Department of Criminal Justice at the University of Houston. His scholarly interests include victimization and sexual violence, especially among inmates.

Kristine Levan is associate professor in the Department of Criminal Justice at Plymouth State University. She is author of *Prison Violence: Causes, Consequences, and Solutions* and has published articles in *Justice Quarterly* and *International Journal of Criminology and Sociological Theory.*

Catherine D. Marcum is assistant professor of justice studies at Appalachian State University. Her research focuses on correctional issues, sexual victimization, and cybercrime offending and victimization.

Danielle McDonald is associate professor of criminal justice at Northern Kentucky University. Her primary areas of research and teaching are reentry programs, corrections, substance abuse, program evaluation, and service learning.

Alexis Miller is associate professor in the Department of Political Science and Criminal Justice at Northern Kentucky University. Her research interests include race and crime, hate crimes, prisoners' rights, criminal justice students, the juvenile death penalty, crime and the media, and institutional corrections.

Janet L. Mullings is executive director of Sam Houston State University–The Woodlands Center and professor in the College of Criminal Justice there. Her research and teaching interests include long-term consequences of victimization, family violence, prison organizations, and women offenders.

Roberto Hugh Potter is professor and director of research partnerships in the Department of Criminal Justice at the University of Central Florida. Previously, he worked at the Centers for Disease Control and Prevention where, among other things, he was part of the Corrections and Substance Abuse Unit at the National Center for HIV, Viral Hepatitis, STD, and TB Prevention.

Jeffrey Rosky is assistant professor in the Department of Criminal Justice at the University of Central Florida. His research interests include criminological theory, correctional treatment programs, and research methods.

Richard Tewksbury is professor of justice administration at the University of Louisville. Previously, he served as research director for the national Prison Rape Elimination Commission. His research focuses on issues of criminal victimization, correctional institution culture and management, gendered experiences, and sexual assault.

Barbara Zaitzow is professor of criminal justice at Appalachian State University. She conducts research projects in men's and women's prisons and has been involved in local, state, and national advocacy work for prisoners and organizations seeking alternatives to imprisonment. She has published extensively on a variety of prison-related topics, including HIV/AIDS and other treatment needs of women prisoners and the impact of prison culture on the "doing time" experiences of the imprisoned.

Index

About the Book

Despite being deemed an illegal activity, participation in sexual activity behind prison walls is a frequent occurrence. Catherine Marcum and Tammy Castle provide a comprehensive study of all aspects of prison sex.

Incorporating inmate, correctional officer, and policymaker perspectives—and debunking myths—the authors consider the full range of consensual and nonconsensual behaviors. They also address the physical, emotional, and legal repercussions of participating in prison sexual relationships. Their analysis is enriched by a case study of a privately run correctional facility, revealing the effects of the Prison Rape Elimination Act at the local level.

Catherine D. Marcum is assistant professor of justice studies at Appalachian State University. **Tammy L. Castle** is associate professor of justice studies at James Madison University.